WRITERS AND POLITICS
IN MODERN SCANDINAVIA

Writers and Politics
in Modern Scandinavia

Janet Mawby

HOLMES & MEIER PUBLISHERS, INC.
NEW YORK

Writers and Politics in Modern Scandinavia is one of a series of books under the general editorship of Professor John Flower. The other books in the series are as follows:

Writers and Politics in Modern Britain (J. A. Morris)
Writers and Politics in Modern France (J. E. Flower)
Writers and Politics in Modern Germany (C. E. Williams)
Writers and Politics in Modern Italy (J. A. Gart-Rutter)
Writers and Politics in Modern Spain (J. Butt)
Writers and Politics in Modern Russia (M. A. Nicholson)

First published in the United States of America 1978 by
Holmes & Meier Publishers, Inc.
30 Irving Place, New York, N.Y. 10003

Library of Congress Cataloging in Publication Data

Mawby, Janet.
  Writers and politics in modern Scandinavia.

  Bibliography: p.
  1. Scandinavian literature—20th century—History and criticism.
  2. Authors, Scandinavian—20th century—Political and social views.
  3. Politics and literature.
  4. World War, 1939-1945—Literature and the war.
  I. Title.
  PT7078.M3   839'.5'0904   78-18931

ISBN 0-8419-0417-0

Printed in Great Britain.

Foreword

The term 'political literature' like 'committed literature' with which it is frequently associated has become an accepted part of the language of literary history. Yet, however convenient, it is, on examination, surprisingly imprecise and misleading. The whole area of the interaction between politics and literature is a vast and complex one which has yet, especially on a European scale, to be fully and comprehensively charted. Certainly invaluable contributions do already exist: Jean-Paul Sartre's *Qu'est-ce que la littérature?* (1947), George Woodcock's *The Writer and Politics* (1948), Jürgen Rühle's *Literatur und Revolution* (1960), Irving Howe's *Politics and the Novel* (1961), John Mander's *The Writer and Commitment* (1961) for example. There are, too, as the bibliographical information contained in the individual essays in this series will reveal, a number of equally important books which deal with the issue in purely national terms. With few exceptions, however, these, like many of the more general studies, suffer from the same defects resulting in the main from a failure to distinguish adequately between 'political literature' and what might be termed 'social literature', and from an incomplete assessment of changes both in political climates and in the writer's relationship to society as a whole. Yet, even when the area of investigation and terminology has been more carefully ascertained, we often find that these books are principally concerned either with an examination of the political ideas *per se* contained in various works of literature, or with an assessment of the ways in which parties and movements have controlled and used to best advantage writers and intellectuals who claim political allegiance. More recently Roland Barthes in *Le Degré Zéro de l'écriture* (1967), George Steiner in *Language and Silence* (1967) and David Caute in *The Illusion* (1971) have suggested a wider perspective, outlining some of the problems of style and form which an imaginative writer has to face when he offers his pen to a political (or social) cause. On the whole, however, it is fair to say that the majority of critics have concentrated more on *what* ideas are expressed than on *how* they have been. In addition therefore to attempting to define the concept of political literature more precisely and to exploring such issues as the suitability of imaginative literature as a vehicle for political ideas or the effect such literature can have on the public for example, one of the principal concerns of these essays is to attempt to examine ways in which an author's political sympathy or affiliation can be seen to affect or even dictate the way in which he writes. In some countries – in Russia, France or Spain, for example – direct influence of this kind is more apparent than in others. Elsewhere, notably in Britain, where political directives concerning art and literature have not been the rule, the problem is in some ways more difficult to assess. Indeed national variation of this kind is one of the principal contributory factors to the complex nature of the whole question. Thus while the subject is best illustrated and examined in the literature of France and Germany during the interwar years, it is after the Second World War that it fully emerges in the works of Italian and Scandinavian writers. Furthermore literary experiment seen and approved in some countries as an expression of a progressive, even revolutionary, political position is considered in others to be characteristic of subversion and decadence.

Given such problems as these and given too the amount of space available, this series of short essays can do little more than hope to encourage a new approach to political literature. While free to explore the subject in the way they believe to be most useful within the context of the literary history of their particular countries, contributors have been encouraged to balance general comment with examination of specific examples. Inevitably therefore the essays appear arbitrarily selective. But like the literature which they choose to examine it is hoped that they will be judged not only for what they contain but also for the ways in which they deal with it.

John Flower

General Bibliography

The following are a selection of those books which discuss some of the general problems associated with this subject.

BARTHES, Roland, *Le Degré Zéro de l'écriture*, Editions du Seuil, Paris, 1953 (Translated: *Writing Degree Zero*, Cape, London, 1967.)

CAUTE, David, *The Illusion: An Essay on Politics, Theatre and the Novel*, Deutsch, London, 1971.

CROSSMAN, Richard, *The God that Failed: Six Studies in Communism*, Hamish Hamilton, London, 1950.

HOWE, Irving, *Politics and the Novel*, Horizon Press, New York, 1955.

MANDER, John, *The Writer and Commitment*, Secker & Warburg, London, 1961.

MUIR, Edwin, *Essays on Literature and Society*, Hogarth Press, London, 1965.

PANICHAS, George, A. (ed.), *The Politics of Twentieth-Century Novelists*, Crowell, New York, 1974.

RÜHLE, Jürgen, *Literatur und Revolution*, Kiepenheuer & Witsch, 1960. (Translated: *Literature and Revolution*, Pall Mall, London, 1969.)

SARTRE, Jean-Paul, *Qu'est-ce que la littérature?* Gallimard, Paris, 1948. (Translated: *What is Literature?* Methuen, London, 1951).

STEINER, George, *Language and Silence: Essays and Notes, 1958-66*, Faber, London, 1967.

TROTSKY, Leon, *Literature and Revolution*, University of Michigan Press, Ann Arbor, 1960.

WINEGARTEN, Renee, *Writers and Revolution: the fatal lure of action*, Franklin Watts, New York, 1974.

WOODCOCK, George, *The Writer and Politics*, The Porcupine Press, London, 1948.

Contents

Introduction

It is difficult to say when the connection between literature and politics began in Scandinavia. In the widest sense, that of presenting a personal view of a society ruled by certain laws and conventions and of influencing the mind of the reader in a certain direction, literature has of course always been a political act. Yet even in the somewhat narrower sense (the sense which I shall use here), that of being composed by a writer who views a society, usually his own, with a consciously appraising eye and with the intention of expressing judgements about its functioning and its effect on its members, politically-orientated literature has existed since the earliest times, and writers have been taken seriously as political influences. One can certainly find such comment and such motivation in the Icelandic sagas, and that most well-known of saga-writers, Snorri Sturluson, composed his works in the interval of complicated intrigues which eventually led to a violent death. Since then, too, many authors have used their writings as comment and even as weapons in a political fight. But these tend to be isolated figures; Scandinavian writers as a group have not really been aware of their political significance until this century – or, at least, until the last decades of last century, when many followed the appeal of the radical Danish critic Georg Brandes to use literature as a forum for debate and looked more closely at the actual fabric of their own society and the threadbare patches of inequality and injustice. Social and political awareness went hand in hand.

In the twentieth century there are many groups of writers whose works could fruitfully be studied with a view to exploring the shaping influence of their political ideas on their creative talent. Often such a group has as its organ a magazine, such as *Mot Dag* and *Profil* in Norway, *Heretica* and *Dialog* in Denmark, *Clarté* and *Rondo* in Sweden. Each of these bodies contained at one time or another writers with a largely common ideology and provided a vehicle for the development of their ideas and for reciprocal influences. And there are other periods than the ones I have chosen which provide ample material in this connection, such as the 1930s, with their proletarian and collective novels, their echoes of international crises and the growing unease at the threat of Fascism, both at home and abroad.

In order to avoid presenting a mere catalogue of works, I find myself compelled to limit the scope of this essay severely. Thus I have

3

chosen to concentrate on two specific periods in which the relationship between literature and politics has been at its closest and in which, for different reasons, the spheres of interest of a variety of writers have coincided most nearly. First, I shall discuss the impact of the Second World War and the German occupation of Norway and Denmark on the writers of those two countries; and second, the 'politicisation of literature' which occurred in Sweden during the latter part of the 1960s in conjunction with the growth of protest about the war in Vietnam and a heightened consciousness of the realities behind the facade of Western democracy.

In a study of committed literature in Scandinavia in any modern period, the main emphasis must fall on the literature of the left. Right-wing authors are often in favour of the *status quo* and are therefore not interested in provoking any political action on the part of the reader; they do not seek to convert, merely to lull into passivity. The few committed authors of the right who are more energetic in their address to the reader, such as Valdemar Rørdam and Finn Halvorsen, are very little read, and therefore their works have no significant influence and are indeed often difficult to obtain. Hamsun is the one right-wing author who stands out as being both actively in favour of change and certainly still read; but he is a lone figure, who has been studied with enthusiasm by many political opponents without causing them to modify their views. His influence in that field is as small as in other fields it is great. With this exception, however, almost all literature of any significance with political intent has been produced by the left.

When considering Scandinavian literature in a European context, it is important to bear in mind the special position of the three Scandinavian countries under discussion. Geographically as well as politically they have been somewhat isolated, in the earlier years of this century at least; because of their policy of neutrality, all three countries have produced writers with a peculiar awareness of being 'committed' in an 'uncommitted' society. Theirs is the dilemma of too much freedom rather than too little. These problems were simplified for Norwegian and Danish writers during the Second World War, when there was an obvious stand to be taken and involvement, despite the cost, brought a curious relief; in Sweden, the malaise was intensified, and a mood of self-accusation and 'bad conscience', which is in part the basis of the self-critical nature of the literature I shall examine, spread rapidly. In the literature of all three countries, there is a persistent feeling of being specially privileged, of watching the suffering from outside – the writer as a parasite in a parasitic society.

4

Chapter One

Norway and Denmark:
The Second World War

The non-involvement of Scandinavia in the First World War and its declared intention of neutrality in the Second* gave the sudden German occupation of Norway and Denmark on 9 April 1940 a stunning impact: stunning in military terms – Denmark put up practically no resistance, and though there was bitter fighting in Norway it was disorganised and the troops were ill-equipped and never had any real chance – and stunning too in psychological terms. The Resistance, and the underground literature which went with it, were slow to become properly organised; people were so totally unprepared. Conditions differed somewhat in the two countries during the first part of the occupation. In Norway, it was a military occupation from the start – the king and government fled abroad, and there was little attempt to disguise the fact that the country was under direct German rule. A strict censorship was immediately imposed; the press and publishing firms became organs of propaganda for the new Germany, and the penalties for writing and printing subversive literature were severe – the Germans were well aware of the power of the printed word.

To Denmark the Germans came as *en venligsindet stat* (a friendly power), expressing the intention of protecting without interfering. The king and government were left in nominal control of the country, and to begin with there was a certain amount of tolerance. Within limits, newspapers and publishers were free to print what they wanted, and life changed little on the surface. But from the end of 1942 the situation deteriorated rapidly until the Germans took over completely after August 1943, ruling by open terror there as in Norway.

The differing situations of the two countries are reflected in the literature produced during the occupation and in the illegal press which emerged in both. In Norway, where radios were confiscated in the autumn of 1941, many of the illegal publications were devoted

---

*That is, political neutrality; economically all the countries have been accused of being far from neutral in either war, as for example in Nordahl Grieg's *Vår ære og vår makt* (1935).

simply to spreading the news from London and discussing the facts of the situation, as a counterbalance to German propaganda. The main literary genre to flourish under these conditions was poetry, especially that of Arnulf Øverland, Nordahl Grieg, Gunnar Reiss-Andersen, who wrote short poems which were easy to distribute and quick to memorise, with uncomplicated patriotic appeal and regular, insistent rhythms. An example is Grieg's *Øya i ishavet*:

> Mørk står en øy av hav,
> ensom og kald og bar.
> Dette er Norges land.
> Dette er alt vi har.
> (*An island rises darkly from the sea,*
> *lonely and cold and bare.*
> *This is the land of Norway.*
> *This is all we have.*)

Longer works, such as novels, were most often written later, in more reflective mood; and those which were written during the war did not have the same sharp appeal to action as the poetry. For obvious reasons they were less easy to distribute through illegal channels. Very few which made any comments on the situation were published legally during the war, and even those had to disguise their criticism in some way, leaving it to the reader to make the connection (Vesaas, *Kimen*, 1940). Books which were more directly critical were held back for publication after the war or were sometimes published in Sweden (Johan Borgen, *Ingen sommer*, 1944; Paal Brekke, *Fri är du född*, 1943).

Danish authors too sometimes smuggled their works to Sweden for publication there (Hans Scherfig, *Idealister*, 1944; Ole Juul, *De røde Enge*, 1945; Otto Gelsted, *Jøderne i Husaby*, 1944); but much was published in Denmark itself, both legally and illegally, including books which would never have been allowed to appear in Norway, even though they were often immediately banned (Soya: *En Gæst*, 1941; Kelvin Lindemann: *Den kan vel Frihed bære*, 1943; Kaj Munk: *Niels Ebbesen*, 1942). In Denmark, too, the underground press printed poems, among them those of Halfdan Rasmussen and Morten Nielsen, as well as much of the work of the author-priest Kaj Munk (sermons, essays and the play *Før Cannae*, 1943) and a collection of stories, poems and articles by many (anonymous) authors, *Der brænder en Ild* (1944). Disguised criticism which leaked out through the normal channels was often clothed in allegorical form or made 'innocuous' by being transplanted to a different historical period.

I shall now look more closely at examples of four kinds of literature produced as a direct response to the occupation: first, the literature of the Resistance, outspoken and immediate in its reaction to events; second, allegorical and historical parallels which commented indirectly; third, realistic novels by authors openly critical of their own society and its failures; and, finally, works which concentrated on the particular problems of the author in wartime and his privileged role. Apart from the first section, my remarks will be concentrated mainly on the novel, as it is arguably the most important genre in the immediate postwar years and certainly the one in which the issues are debated most fully. And I have preferred to look closely at the works of a few authors who are generally accepted as important literary figures in their own right rather than to try to give a picture of the whole field. The war, not surprisingly, produced a spate of committed literature and left some traces in the works of nearly all writers.

The Literature of the Resistance: Nordahl Grieg and Kaj Munk

1. Nordahl Grieg (1902-43)

Nordahl Grieg was a political writer for most of his life and one of the most active of Norwegian writers working abroad during the 1920s and 1930s. A tireless and rapid worker, he studied in Oxford, visited China as a reporter, lived in Russia for two years and was in Spain as an observer during the Civil War. His writing, which began with poems about his adventures as a sailor in his early youth, became more and more obsessed by war and its effect on mankind as the 1930s drew to a close. His attack on Norwegian profiteering during the First World War, *Vår ære og vår makt* (1935), was followed by another play about war, *Nederlaget* (1937) (*Defeat*, 1945), which takes as its subject the Paris Commune of 1870 and the dilemma of a freedom movement whose leaders believe that violence is evil but find themselves forced to resort to violence in order to achieve their free society. This conflict is at the centre both of Grieg's works and of his life and became acute as war approached. Originally a pacifist, he came to realise the necessity of force on certain occasions: 'Godheten kan bare seire ved vold, det er det bitre vi har lært' ('*Goodness can conquer only by means of force; that is the bitter lesson we have learnt*') (*Nederlaget*, p. 98). Politically he became the most left-wing Norwegian author of his time, editing the outspoken anti-Fascist magazine *Veien frem* (1936-7). His Communist sympathies were intensified by his experience of the Spanish Civil War (see *Spansk*

7

sommer, 1937) and his stay in Russia. He was the only Norwegian intellectual to defend Russia during the Moscow show trials – a defence which appears in *Ung må verden ennu være* (1938). This novel contrasts Russian single-mindedness and willingness to pursue the ultimate aim unquestioningly with the vacillating 'humanism' of the Western intellectual ('humanism' became for Grieg a synonym for an ineffectual idealism which has no grasp of the realities of a situation). When the occupation came, he had already joined the army; he helped to smuggle Norway's gold to England, where he subsequently produced poetry, essays and radio talks and took an active part in the war until he was shot down over Berlin in 1943.

Grieg's poetry is rather different from the rest of his creative writing. From his earliest lyrics, he had cultivated a simple, traditional verse form, with clear pictures and a straightforward theme, which contrasts with the sometimes tortuous conflicts of his prose and the ambitious and original scenic effects of his plays. During the 1930s, as he worked out his own doubts, reflecting the turbulent moods of the day, he relied more on other literary forms. On the outbreak of war, he turned again to poetry. The contingencies of the situation demanded an unequivocal response, and for him as for many others poetry was the most effective literary weapon.

His poetry was written, above all, not to be admired as an end in itself but to attain one single goal – freedom for Norway. Gone are the ambiguities and the questioning, gone too the ideological arguments about the merits of various political systems. The patriot and monarchist, always latent in Grieg, are given full rein in poems such as *17 maj 1940*, broadcast from the north of Norway on that day, and *Kongen*, which celebrates the proud self-reliance of the king and the freedom which he gave to all to choose their allegiance.

> Han er mere enn en fører,
> for han trodde på de andre,
> sinnets eget kongerike.
> Mot en *fremtid* skal han gå,
> for han selv har mere *frihet*
> i sitt hjerte enn de fleste.
> Derfor er han folkekongen
> i et land hvor hver skal være
> fører for sin egen skjebne,
> høvding i sitt eget sinn.
> (*Samlede dikt*, pp. 187-8, my italics).
> (*He is more than a leader,*
> *for he believed in others,*

in the kingdom of a man's own mind.
He shall move towards the future,
for he himself has more freedom
in his heart than most.
Therefore he is the people's king
in a country where all shall be
masters of their own fates
rulers of their own minds.)

As in the above stanza, the syntax of these poems is usually simple, depending on main clauses and one or two subordinate clauses, with natural word-order and end-stopped lines. The vocabulary is also limited, words such as *frihet* (freedom) and *fremtid* (future) recurring in nearly every poem and carrying much emotive weight. Battle and nature imagery predominate, the colours are those of blood and of grass, of earth and rocks, of ice and snow. Much of it is poetry for the moment and was not intended to last; and one doubts that Grieg would have expressed the same sentiments in a less extreme situation. He is far from being so complimentary to his compatriots in *Vår ære og vår makt* and *Ung må verden ennu være*, and this poetry is not entirely free of the kind of *krigsromantikk* (romanticising of war) which he condemns in *Nederlaget*:

> *Krigskrøplingen*: Vi har fedrelandet. For det har jeg gitt liv og lemmer, og det skal andre gjøre, de også. *Alle* andre! Vil du vi skal ha lidd forgjeves?
> *Varlin*: Ja, min venn. Helst ville jeg det. Best var det om du ble glemt. For du er æren, lidelsen og neste krig.
> (*Nederlaget*, p. 23-4)
> (The wounded veteran:
> *We have our country. I've given my life and limbs for it, and others must do so too. All the others! Do you want us to have suffered in vain?*
> Varlin:
> *Yes, my friend. That is what I really want. It would be best if you were forgotten. For you stand for honour, suffering and the next war.*)

It is the glory rather than the dirt of the conflict that emerges from the poems, for they were spurs to action rather than recollections in tranquillity. Grieg did not live long enough to express a more dispassionate view after the event; but he did write two poems, *Sjømannen* and *Den menneskelige natur*, which, he instructed, were not to be published until after the war. These show the other side of the heady optimism expressed in the fighting poems. *Sjømannen*, written in July

1942, expresses the bitterness of the weary sailor who is exhorted over the radio to carry on the good fight by those who sit comfortably on land; his is not the glad spirit of sacrifice but the grey, endless toil of a job that must somehow be done.

> Da skal vi likevel seile
> i bitre, frysende år,
> fordi vi kan ikke annet,
> fordi denne krigen er vår . . .
>
> Kjenner du frihetens ansikt?
> Nærm dig og du skal se:
> det er et dødninge-hode.
> Skremmes du bort av det?
> (*Samlede dikt*, p. 217)
> (*Despite all, we shall carry on sailing*
> *through the bitter, freezing years,*
> *because we can't do anything else,*
> *because this is our war . . .*
>
> *Do you know what the face of freedom looks like?*
> *Come closer and you shall see:*
> *it is an empty skull.*
> *Does it frighten you?*)

In *Den menneskelige natur* (written in September 1942), one of Grieg's longest poems, he admits the self-doubt, the moments of despair which he excluded from his Resistance poems, and departs altogether from glorification of his own countrymen. The enemy in the long term is not the Germans but a certain kind of man who is to be found on both sides – the kind of man who thinks war is a part of human nature and blithely accepts the suffering of others as the natural order of things. Against this Grieg asserts his belief in the ultimate power of man to control his own destiny – but to be effective the power must be continually exerted. Apathy means defeat, and the enemy never rests.

From these more complex, less confident poems it becomes clear that Nordahl Grieg was not suddenly converted into a simple idealistic patriot by the coming of war to his own land. Yet the pressure of his restlessly questioning intellect was partly relieved during the battle as he used his literary talents in the service of a temporarily more urgent need. The literary quality of the Resistance poems is not always high; nor was it important to their author – there would be time for aesthetic considerations, as for doubts and recriminations, after Norway had been freed.

2. Kaj Munk (1898-1944)

Although Kaj Munk was a writer far removed from Nordahl Grieg both in temperament and in political convictions, their paths drew closer during the occupation, and both met their death in the struggle against Germany.

Munk stands out as a strange, lone figure in the Danish literature of the 1920s and 1930s. A priest who spent his whole working life in Vedersø, a bleak country community on the west coast of Jutland, he was also a fierce polemicist, who kept his eye on European developments, and an innovatory dramatist who, though initially received negatively by the critics, eventually established himself as one of the few outstanding Danish playwrights of this century. From the early days he combined a determined commitment to Christianity with an ardent admiration of the strong man, the dictator, whom he saw as the prime mover of history and the urgently-needed saviour of the modern world. The duality, sometimes conflict, of these two ideals dominates his writings. In one of his earliest plays, *En Idealist* (1924) (*Herod the King*, 1953), the central figure is that of the tyrant Herod, a man strong in evil, who is confronted by the baby Jesus and capitulates; he is not strong enough, and his love for his wife Mariamme is the weakness which finally destroys him.

Munk hailed the dictator as the man who would rouse Europe – and, he hoped, Denmark – from their apathy. His essays and articles during the 1930s contain a mixture of admiration for Hitler and Mussolini ('snart det eneste sunde Mandfolk i Europa, der kan handle', *Aabent Brev til Mussolini*, 17/11/38 – *'just about the only real man in Europe who can get something done'*, Open Letter to Mussolini) and appeals to Denmark to take a stronger line herself and not to be intimidated by outsiders. Yet his open praise of the Italian and German leaders was motivated more by an idealistic cult of personality than by any political allegiance to their doctrines. Although right-wing in many of his views, Munk remained an individualist without any definite party commitment. He could certainly not be described as a Fascist; he spoke out against any attempt by the dictators to impose their ideas and their way of life on other races and other countries. He condemned the treatment of the Jews and the occupation of Czechoslovakia. Munk's doubts about the abuse of power can be seen in a play written just before the war, *Han sidder ved Smeltediglen* (1938) (*He sits at the Melting-Pot*, 1953), in which he attacks anti-Semitism, at the same time showing his unwillingness to abandon his former feelings for the *Führer*; he is 'saa nær ved at være en Gud, som det er muligt, naar han dog blot er et Menneske' (*'as close to being a god as is possible when he is only human after all') (Egelykke og andre Skuespil, p. 37).*

As the political situation became unmistakably clear after 9 April 1940, the conflict between his pro-Hitlerism and his fears for the safety of Denmark was resolved. This can be seen most starkly in his poetry, which became prolific during the last four years of his life, as indeed in his other writing too. In drama, verse, articles and sermons he poured out his energies in an unremitting attack on the invader and exhortations to his fellow Danes. And now it was to the people he turned, not to a leader; the best of his country became for him the ordinary folk, as in *Samfundsstøtter*.

> Men aldrig slettes Danmarks Navn,
> saa længe som i København
> er endnu ikke ryddet ud
> det allersidste Cyklebud. . . .
>
> Og hør, I jydske Tjennestpi'er,
> dernæst er I vort Riges Sir.
> Det staar, saalænge, si'er jeg jer,
> som I er saadan, som I er.
> *(Digte, pp. 218-19)*
> *(But Denmark's name will never be wiped out*
> *as long as in Copenhagen*
> *there is still left*
> *one last remaining errand boy on a cycle. . . .*
>
> *And you, you servant girls from Jutland,*
> *you are the next most precious ornament of our kingdom.*
> *It will stand as long, I tell you,*
> *as you remain the way you are.)*

Munk's genius undoubtedly reached fuller expression in his drama than in his poetry, which is often distinguished more by its enthusiasm than by any literary qualities. As in this passage, the metre is usually banal and the choice of rhyme often unconvincing.

Munk published his writings, legally when he could, illegally when he could not, throughout the occupation until he was shot by the Germans as a reprisal for Danish Resistance activity in January 1944. His theme was nearly always the same: once his theoretical deliberations had been resolved by the physical presence of an enemy, he became, like Grieg, less interested in ideologies than in making an effective contribution to the fight against oppression. But he did not abandon his favourite form, the drama; his last important full-length play, *Niels Ebbesen*, appeared in 1942 and was translated into English in 1945. A comparison of this play with the earlier ones I have mentioned demonstrates the distance Munk had travelled. As in his poetry, he abandoned the hunt for a *Führer*; the hero, who gives his name to the play, is not a dictator or even a great leader but a peace-loving Danish farmer who just wants to stay at home and get on with his work. In a clear parallel with the contemporary situation, the country is occupied by Germans, whose demands become more and more strident as more is conceded. Eventually Niels can compromise no more; when the Germans demand Danish soldiers for their army he refuses and kills the German tyrant, Grev Gert. But he makes his decision without striking any noble stance or undergoing any sudden transformation from his normal unheroic self. He acts with fear and hesitation, but he does act, and with the voluntary support of his fellow-countrymen; the solidarity of the group triumphs over the lonely power of the tyrant.

Munk's final dramatic comment on the theme of the dictator, the one-act *Før Cannae* (1943) (*Before Cannae*, 1953), portrays an invented meeting between Hannibal and the Roman general Fabius Cunctator. His sympathy clearly lies with Fabius, the wise old man whose policy is to avoid bloodshed whenever possible and to let children go on playing in the streets of both Rome and Carthage, and against the war-lord Hannibal, who leads his people to glory and annihilation.

> *Fabius*: Du anser mig for en gammel Idiot. Du har Ret; det er jeg utvivlsomt. Det samme regner de mig for hjemme i Rom. Og det er det tillidvækkende ved mig. Du, Hannibal, du er et Geni; det anerkender vi alle, og vi takker Jupiter for, at du ikke er født hos os. Den værste Skæbne, der kan overgaa et Folk, er at blive hjemsøgt af et Geni.
>
> (*Egelykke og andre Skuespil*, p. 297)
> (Fabius: *You regard me as an old idiot. You're right; there's no doubt that I am. That's what they think of me back home in Rome too. And that's what makes people trust me. You, Hannibal, you're a genius; we all recognise that, and we thank Jupiter that you weren't born one of us. The worst fate that can befall a race is to be afflicted by a genius.*)

Under the pressure of the political events of his day, Munk moved from celebrating the achievements of a superman to unremitting opposition to the heroic ideal in the name of freedom for the masses the dictator would enslave.

For both Munk and Grieg, the occupation came, in the literary sense, as something of a relief; the literary discussion of ideological conflicts gave way to a more single-minded commitment to a definite end, in which creative writing was only one of the weapons. For other writers, matters did not become so simple; indeed, for some the conflicts were intensified rather than resolved.

Images of conflict: Tarjei Vesaas and Hans Kirk

The difficulties a watchful censorship put in the way of broadcasting any comment on the occupation made writers ever more adroit in clothing their remarks in seemingly innocent garb and made readers more sensitive to half-hinted allusions hidden between the lines. Often the veiled references were made where the Germans would least expect them: in the daily press they came not in the serious articles (which were mainly propaganda) but in the light-hearted *kåserier* (anecdotes) of Johan Borgen, *Mumle Gåsegg*, which appeared in the Oslo newspaper *Dagbladet* as little sketches of everyday life but concealed a telling point or an encouraging assurance, and in the *Gruk* of Piet Hein, humorous poems published daily in *Politiken* which took a wry look at events. Perhaps the best-known is Hein's description of an orchestra, which by means of several puns contrives to express doubt about the friendly intentions of the tactful occupation force.

> Et venligsindet Orkester
> ta'r Stade ved Raadhusets Fod.
> Snart samler der sig en Del Mennesker,
> der staar og tænker paa no'ed.
> Det er denne dragende,
> denne rentud besættende Magt,
> og saa er der noget betagende
> ved dette Opbud af Takt.
> (*A friendly orchestra*
> *takes up its station by the Town Hall.*
> *Soon a number of people gather,*
> *they're standing and thinking about something.*
> *It's this compelling,*
> *this absolutely captivating power,*
> *and then there is something moving*
> *about this display of rhythm.*)

('Venligsindet', friendly, was the official description of the German occupying forces. 'En besættende Magt' means both a captivating power and an occupying force, and 'Takt' means both rhythm and tact.)

14

Many works of literature written during the war discussed what was happening in other terms. A favourite method was to use some image for the state of society – as the house in Tarjei Vesaas' *Huset i mørkret*, for instance, and the ship in Hans Kirk's *Slaven* – or to show human qualities reflected in the animal world – as in the pigs in Vesaas' *Kimen*. The use of animal stories to comment on human behaviour was especially popular in Denmark, where the message was often carried by an insect. Soya's *En Gæst* is the story of a strange earwig which is accepted into a family and gradually grows until it fills the whole house (a parallel which was perhaps rather too obvious, as the book was banned at once). Classical tales were revived and found to have new meaning in a new context (e.g. H. C. Andersen's *De små grønne*); and Gunnar Helweg-Larsen's fearful tale of *Bøgenonne-larverne* (moth grubs) ravaging the green forests of South Jutland, soon to be overcome by the natural resistance which takes the form of a fungus, is unambiguous in its reference. Kjeld Abell used an insect image to make his point in *Myrer og Modsigelseslyst*, in which he expressed the hope that people would soon stop behaving like ants and start standing up for themselves.

Historical parallels were the other main source of comparison: accounts of previous periods of invasion and occupation could shed light on contemporary strife and suggest ways of resisting which had been effective before. Munk's *Niels Ebbesen* and *Før Cannae* have already been discussed; Mogens Klitgaard's *De røde Fjer* portrays the English attack on Copenhagen in 1807 and Kelvin Lindemann's *Den kan vel Frihed bære* the Swedish occupation of Bornholm in 1658-9.

1. Tarjei Vesaas (1897-1970)

Imagery and comparisons drawn from the natural world were always a central feature of the works of Tarjei Vesaas. The main themes in his pre-war novels are those of the earth and the harmony of nature. The farm is the centre of his fictional universe and stands for the natural order which triumphs over all evil; even when the central character rebels against it, as does Per in *Det store spelet* (1934), it is a temporary revolt only, and he soon accepts his role in the great cycle. Vesaas' fictional works of the 1930s are almost all in this vein; apart from a short play from the first half of the decade, *Ultimatum* (1934), there is little trace in his fictional works of his forebodings of the darkness to come.

The occupation brought no pause in Vesaas' production. Indeed, he wrote furiously and completed several novels which were not all published until quite some time after the war. Yet there was a marked change of emphasis in his writing after 9 April 1940. From this date his works reflect a deeper concern with the specific problems of violence and evil. Of course there is an overlap from his earlier works; the change is not total. The theme of natural growth is central to *Kimen* and *Tårnet* (1948), for example, and the experience of human contact is, as always, the solution of disharmony. It is rather the atmosphere of the works that changed; it grew darker, more pessimistic in some ways and above all more committed.

Kimen, which was published as early as the autumn of 1940 (*The Seed*, 1966), shows how swiftly Vesaas reacted to events. In a preface written for the 1967 Norwegian Book Club edition he underlined the close relationship between the novel and the German invasion.

> Ein måtte famle og prøve skaffe seg utløysing nokoleis. Det fall av seg sjølv at det ein prøvde forme, vart om villskap, fornedring, samvet, audmyking, og om, kanskje, oppreising. . . . I rekka av bøkene mine står *Kimen* som eit deleteikn. *Det* var ikkje planlagt, men noko så opprivande og utruleg var skjedd, at det førde med seg ny skrivemåte, utan vidare. . . . Einslags annan måte å kjenne tinga på.
>
> (*You had to try, tentatively, to find some kind of outlet for your feelings. It happened quite naturally that what you tried to formulate was about violence, degradation, conscience, humiliation, and perhaps, too, about regeneration. . . . In the progression of my books,* Kimen *represents a fundamental break. That was not planned, but something so shattering and incredible had happened, that it automatically led to a new way of writing. . . . A different kind of way of feeling things.*)

With such an introduction, it is natural to read *Kimen* as a war novel, though, like nearly all of Vesaas' work, it is capable of a much more general interpretation. Vesaas is not a political commentator in the narrow sense; and, indeed, the fact that the novel was published openly in 1940 indicates that it can be read as a work of literature unconnected with actual historical fact. The Second World War was the occasion and the spur, but it was also just one example of how the conflicts described are acted out in society.

The central theme of the novel is the problem of violence: how it originates and how it is passed on. On a green and peaceful island, a chain of violence is formed and communicated from one mind to another like a kind of madness, in the animal as well as the human world. The old boar crashes about his sty in a raging fury; two sows catch the mood and fight to the death; another sow eats her own

16

young. The natural process of creation becomes a self-destructive nightmare. This is witnessed by Andreas, who is the human agent of destruction. His mind has been unbalanced by an explosion at a chemical factory, in which he saw many innocent dead, and he has come to the island in a restless search for mental harmony through contact with nature; his search ends in the sty of the sow who is eating her young. This experience makes him lose what little control he has over his actions. He murders a young girl he meets by chance and is in his turn murdered by her brother Rolv, who leads a hysterical mob which tears Andreas to pieces. But here, finally, the chain of violence is broken; through a night of watching by the dead man's body, the islanders repent and atone. Rolv is saved from despair by the strength of his bond with his family – he has the vital contact with others which Andreas lacked. The harmony of nature reasserts itself; Gudrun, the murdered girl's friend, is expecting a baby and the island is still green. Human nature can conquer the evil which is inherent in it, though in *Kimen* the threat is seen as much stronger than in Vesaas' earlier novels. There, violence is essentially under control, contained like the waters behind the dam in the *Dyregodt* novels; here, the force of destruction is released, and the victory is by no means assured.

The darkness is more oppressive and more permanent in *Huset i mørkret* (1945) (*The House in the Dark*, 1976), written during the last few months of the war, after several years of occupation. For the first and only time in Vesaas' novels, nature is excluded; the action takes place within a large house with endless, dark corridors ruled over by an invisible but all-seeing enemy who sits right in the centre and has the power of life and death over the inhabitants. The parallels with the occupation are more direct than in *Kimen*, and the people who live in the house represent all kinds of reaction to the foreign dictatorship: Stig, the Resistance worker who carries on doggedly with the seemingly hopeless fight and accepts imprisonment and torture rather than trying to save himself; Martin, the stamp collector who tries to shut his ears and eyes to what is happening with the justification that he is working for the future; *pilpussaren*, the man who polishes the enemy's golden arrows which draw people towards the centre and who is himself tempted by material gain and a craven admiration of strong men into collaborating; and Stein, the devil-may-care adventurer who joins the Resistance not because it is a necessary but grim task but because it is fun.

Huset i mørkret is certainly a novel about conflict; but taken out of context it can be seen as the description of any society in the grip of a tyrant or even of a mind divided against itself. Like *Kimen*, it is general rather than specific. Vesaas does not endeavour to explain

17

how the whole situation came about, who is responsible for the present state of the house, what is happening outside or what is to happen afterwards. It is a static novel; we are presented with a *fait accompli*, and there is no release at the end – just a vague hope of future freedom. Vesaas is not interested in recriminations against individuals or in party politics; his is a psychological study which does not apportion blame but tries to understand how all reactions are possible, to explore the tensions created by a situation in which what had previously seemed to be small variations of personality suddenly become the difference between a hero and a traitor. There is no black-and-white distinction between the two sides – the Resistance workers are not entirely heroic and self-sacrificing. In this study of the use of violence, Vesaas draws a fine distinction: it is the attitude of mind that is all-important, not the act itself. Violence is necessary in such a situation, but it is wrong in the hands of men such as Stein because his attitude is wrong, even though he may seem to be on the right side. To use such a man is to descend to the level of the enemy, because he thinks like the enemy – he enjoys destruction, and so in the last analysis he is one of the forces of destruction, in league with those who would destroy the house. In the desperate situation, it is principles such as these that will preserve the house for the day when it is released from the darkness.

2. Hans Kirk (1899-1962)

Hans Kirk was a very different writer from Vesaas; he was a Communist, and his political commitment informed all his writing and coloured his view of the occupation. From his very first novel, *Fiskerne* (1928), he was convinced of the importance of social conditioning and of the way in which men's values, and even their religion, depend on their material circumstances: when a group of people changes its way of life, its ways of thinking are gradually adapted in consequence.

During the 1930s, Kirk wrote novels about the coming of the industrial era and its problems (*Daglejerne*, 1936; *De ny Tider*, 1939). Like Vesaas, at this time he expressed his feelings about contemporary events in articles rather than in fiction. From the former it is clear that he did react strongly to the atmosphere of the decade; he criticised the quasi-Fascist circles of opinion in Denmark as well as pointing out the German danger. Like other Danish Communists, Kirk was more directly and physically affected by the occupation than most civilians; he and many others were arrested by the Danish police 'for their own protection' on June 22 1941 and sent to the prison camp Horserød. By good fortune he escaped in 1943 when the Germans arrived with orders to send all Communists to concentration camps in Germany.

While he was interned during the war Kirk continued studying and writing fiction, and his work from these years bears traces of his growing bitterness at the capitalist system. It is the general evils of capitalism, rather than the specific ones of German Fascism, that he attacks in his political allegory from this time, *Slaven*; Fascism is but the ultimate rationalisation of a society based on oppression and lust for power. Like *Huset i mørkret*, *Slaven* is an image of society containing representatives of the whole social spectrum; the enclosed area is a Spanish ship of the seventeenth century on its way home from the colonies loaded with gold. It is thus removed in time as well as in theme from the contemporary scene – a harmless enough subject for Kirk even to have been allowed to borrow books on it from the university library while he was sitting in prison for his Communist views. The novel was finished during the war but was lost after Kirk's escape and had to be rewritten before it was published in 1948. Its message, though not directly subversive, is far from harmless in its implications. The society on board the ship is evil, ruled by fear and greed masquerading as idealism and brotherly love, and the only free man on board is a slave, a noble savage who comes from a primitive Communist state which has been plundered by marauding capitalists. It is he who finally sinks the ship of capitalism, going down with it rather than accepting the loss of his freedom.

Kirk's next novel, *Vredens Søn* (1950), is also a historical novel written primarily as a comment on the modern conflict, although in this novel the parallel with the occupation is much more direct. It is an account of the life and teachings of Christ, demonstrating Kirk's belief in the fundamental similarity between the ideals of Christianity and those of Communism. The first Christians are shown to be equally the first Communists. And the reaction towards them of the powers that be is prophetic of that of a twentieth-century imperialist state. Jerusalem is under Roman occupation, and those in power are concerned only that everything should remain peaceful, and that clashes which might make things worse should be avoided. Caiaphas sounds remarkably like a cautious Danish minister advising co-operation.

> Vi ligger som en lille klat mennesker midt i det uhyre romerrige, og det er et under, at vi ikke allerede er opslugt helt. Hvad har vi andet at gøre end at samarbejde med besættelsesmagten, at bøje os og samtidig prøve at redde, hvad reddes kan? (p. 94)

(We are just a little clump of people stuck in the middle of the huge Roman empire, and it's a miracle that we're not already swallowed up. What else can we do but collaborate with the occupying forces, make concessions and at the same time try to save what can be saved?)

The Romans regard us as 'et latterligt lille folk' (*'a ridiculous little people'*) (p. 94); but since they allow us 'et vist selvstyre' (*'a certain amount of self-government'*), let us try to keep that by not offending them!

As in *Huset i mørkret*, the whole scala of attitudes to an invader is shown in *Vredens Søn*. The Sadducees believe in energetic *rapprochement*, whereas the people wait passively to be freed but dare not do anything themselves. The Zealots are for active resistance and see in Jesus their leader. Judas is an intellectual who dreams of action, and when Jesus will not give him action he changes sides and tries in vain to justify his reasoning to himself. Jesus is a folk leader who suffers from indecision, a freedom-fighter who is not sure enough of himself to lead an open revolt. His role is seen from a sociological standpoint: he is dangerous, Caiaphas remarks, not because he is the son of God but because he preaches revolution to the poor.

> Han går løs på selve samfundets fundament, han ophidser de usleste i samfundet med løfter om at give dem part i tilværelsens goder. Det er sin sag, hvis en opvigler lover de fattige frihed, men frihed er dog noget forholdsvis abstrakt. Det bliver alvor, når han lover dem mad, for sult og elendighed er noget, som småfolk har inde på livet og ved, hvad er. (p. 119)
> *(He attacks society's very foundations, he excites the most wretched elements of society by promising to give them a share of the good things of life. It's all very well for an agitator to promise freedom to the poor; freedom is at least a fairly abstract sort of thing. But it starts to get really serious when he promises them food, because hunger and misery are something the lower classes have actually experienced; they know what it means.)*

Like not a few Danes, Caiaphas has a certain sympathy for freedom-fighters – provided that they are not Communists.

It is finally not Jesus but the practical Simon who assesses the situation correctly. Jesus relied too much on God; a man must rely first of all on himself. Jesus failed in his efforts, but he was only the first, and many more will come after him. The fight is still the same under the German occupation as it was under the Roman – and there is still a long way to go. By using the Biblical story, Kirk provides Communism with as long a tradition as Christianity itself and attempts to demonstrate that Communism does in fact incorporate the ideals on which our society is supposed to be based. The message is implicit in the story, though the moral is perhaps a little over-stated: Simon's comments at the end, like those of don Pablo in *Slaven*, are rather sophisticated and theoretical – both speak with a historical hindsight which makes them sound like mouthpieces for Kirk rather than voices from their own time.

After these two historical comparisons with his own society, Kirk did turn to a more direct attack. Indignant not only about the events of the occupation but also about the post-war 'retribution', he depicted the facts as he saw them, slightly fictionalised, in *Djævelens Penge*. (1951) and *Klitgaard og Sønner* (1952). Although very little read now and generally considered to be insignificant parts of Kirk's literary production, they represent what he himself thought he ought to be writing as direct political literature. Using rather obvious techniques of rhetoric and grotesque caricature, they are intended as didactic commentaries on historical fact rather than creative writing.

The hidden enemy: Hans Scherfig and Sigurd Hoel

Novels about the Second World War are still being published in Scandinavia. Of those authors who experienced the occupation, nearly all have written something on the subject, which indeed often provided the incentive for a first novel (Jens Bjørneboe: *Før hanen galer*, 1952, and Tage Skou-Hansen: *De nøgne Træer*, 1957, for instance). There are of course many war novels in which the Norwegians or Danes are automatically heroes and the villains Germans; but these are often little different from those produced in any country after a war, and I shall not discuss them here. I now want to look at novels published in Norway and Denmark after the occupation which attempt to give a realistic picture of events as the author saw them, taking into account the special problems which existed in his environment. I shall take as examples two authors who, in different ways, take a critical look at the weaknesses which were revealed in their own society.

1. Hans Scherfig (1905-)

Hans Scherfig is an author who unites two seemingly disparate talents: he is a satirist who delights in poking fun at the foibles of human nature and a Communist who takes his society to task for its injustice and hypocrisy. In his early novels (*Den forsvundne Fuldmægtig*, 1938, and *Det forsømte Forår*, 1940) it is the satirist who is to the fore, though his absurd portrayals of people conditioned by society into accepting roles which have lost any real meaning for them do carry serious social criticism too. But the tone becomes less light-hearted, the accusation more bitter, as first the outbreak of war and then the occupation revealed what in times of peace was hidden beneath a veneer of tolerance. And like the other Danish Communist I have discussed, Hans Kirk, it is in his own society that Scherfig discovered the emergence of Fascism as the logical extension of capitalism at a time of national crisis.

The two novels Scherfig wrote about the approach of war and the war itself are *Idealister* (Sweden, 1944) (*The 'Idealists'*, 1949) and *Frydenholm* (1962). The former gives a picture of Denmark in the 1930s split into quarrelling sects all firmly convinced that they have found salvation; among these pseudo-intellectual short-cuts to a better society the ideology of Nazism is also beginning to spread. Rational thinking is being superseded by whipped-up emotions and primitive urges, and mysticism is coming into its own again. Yet in this novel good-humour still dominates, and criticism is combined with farce. Scherfig treats his idealists with an amused sympathy, and it is only in his comments on the novel (such as those expressed 20 years later in an interview with Niels Birger Wamberg) that the seriousness of his intentions is made unambiguous.

> Fejlen ved alle disse såkaldte idealister er, at de ikke har under-søgt samfundets historie, dets struktur, at de går uden om en videnskabelig samfundsopfattelse og går uden om det afgørende begreb klassekampen.
>
> (*Samtaler med danske Digtere*, p. 54)
> (*The trouble with all these so-called idealists is that they haven't studied the history and structure of society, that they disregard the scientific view of society and ignore the central concept of class conflict.*)

Class conflict, however, appears with much greater force in *Frydenholm*. Gone is the gentleness of Scherfig's ridicule of the mis-guided; the satire is harsh in this detailed indictment of the Danish government and police during the occupation. Events are related in an unemotional style, and the author's pointing finger is not so obvious as it is at times in Kirk's novels; the incredible facts speak for themselves, and the soberly recorded actions of those who appear in the novel already seem stranger than fiction. What the Communists had prophesied had come true to a degree which seemed unbelievable even to them.

Vi har forudsagt det, der sker. Og vi er alligevel forbavsede, når det sker. Det er ligesom, vi ikke rigtig har troet på vores egen teori. Vi har troet på de andre. Det er den fejl, vi har gjort.

(p. 339)

(*We foresaw what is happening now. Yet nevertheless we're amazed when it happens. It's as if we didn't really believe in our own theory. We believed in the others. That's what our mistake has been.*)

Frydenholm is a novel modelled very closely on historical fact. It is easy to find the counterpart of many of the characters in reality, and even the invented characters take part in actual incidents. Attention is concentrated on the persecution of the Communists during the occupation, and a comparison with Kirk's letters in *Fange Nr.6* and the Communist lawyer Carl Madsen's essays in *Den gode Læge* soon shows how little in the account is fictional. Excerpts from Kirk's letters are used in the course of the novel, and incidents experienced by him and Madsen are described. The book is the most complete account there is in novel form of conditions in occupied Denmark. The author is obviously not observing with a dispassionate eye; had it not been for an operation, he would have remained in captivity, and his political convictions increased his indignation against those who contravened the constitution in order to imprison the Communists. Over twenty years after the events concerned, he raised an embarrasing memorial to his country's failure to respond to the challenge of defending its own laws.

2. Sigurd Hoel (1890-1960)

Scherfig looks at his own society and lays the blame for what happened at the door of capitalism. For the Norwegian Sigurd Hoel, however, guilt lies much nearer home. Always a socially aware writer, he was associated with the *Mot Dag* group in the 1920s and campaigned vigorously during the 1930s against the repressive demands of social conformity and authoritarian upbringing; he was also one of the first writers to realise the threat of Nazism and how urgent it was to speak out (see for example *Kulturkamp og litteratur*, 1936). His novel *Sesam Sesam*, written in 1938, is not unlike Scherfig's *Idealister*, a collective view of the contemporary frenzied search for patent medicines to cure the ills of the day, which draws attention to the political and social manipulation to which people are subjected and to the growth of Fascist tendencies as the reactionary elements gather force. Ridicule is also one of his chief weapons, an ironic elegance of style which punctures the pompous utterances of public figures.

The novel which emerged directly from Hoel's war experiences was *Møte ved milepelen* (1947) (*Meeting at the Milestone*, 1951). The first-person narrator of the novel, a man with the imposing nickname of *Den plettfrie* (literally, 'the man without stain') sets out to investigate the reasons why so many of his former fellow-students became Nazis during the war or at least collaborated. And he thinks he finds some kind of answer; they were mostly *bondestudenter*, students from puritanical small-town and country *milieus*, whose strict upbringing condemned love as sin and joy of life as time-wasting; sent to Oslo to study with hardly any money and no guidance, they were left to struggle on with no idea of where they should be going. Crippled by these restrictions at a time when they should have been most free, their energies turned to other outlets, to violence and hatred.

Yet *Den plettfrie* shared these disadvantages, and now during the war he risks his life to help the Resistance and has no links at all with Nazism – or so he thinks. He is soon forced to abandon his position as a moral hero when he discovers that one of the most ruthless Nazis in a town whose Resistance group he helps is in fact his own illegitimate son and that he himself is largely responsible for the fact that this son and the husband of Kari, the woman whom he betrayed, have turned to Nazism. Guilt is no longer something to be apportioned to others – we are all implicated: 'Jeg så nazismen som vårt uekte barn' ('*I saw that Nazism was our own illegitimate child*') (p. 271). The fear instilled into him by his upbringing, fear of sin, fear of being 'trapped' for life, fear of love, made him reject his own child and abandon it to evil. It is the repressive society, in which we in our turn act as repressors, that gives birth to hatred and violence. Hoel realises that he cannot provide a full answer to the question of where the guilt lies and in the novel abandons the attempt to do so for more than one person. But he suggests that it does not always lie where it seems. All evil acts contribute in some way to the sum of evil called Nazism, which for Hoel represents lack of love.

And indeed, Nazism embodies so many of the repressive tendencies abhorrent to Hoel that in this novel it has become the total expression of evil in the world, the incarnation of all our failures and our cowardice. A Nazi is a human being who has not been allowed to develop freely. In an essay written at the same time as this novel, *Om nazismens vesen* (1945), Hoel uses Nazism as a synonym for the social trends he has always opposed. The patriarchal society is the source of Nazi tendencies, and so anything which he connects with this form of society – reaction, repression of women's rights, a puritanical attitude to sex leading to fear of it, the unnecessarily strict education of children, even the over-specialisation of modern academic life   is

24

conducive to Nazism. People are too fond of their own little sties and want security and ignorance rather than knowledge and freedom; and the thirst for political power is a substitute for the love they have lost or have never had.

Møte ved milepelen puts these theories into fictional form – and makes them more convincing through Hoel's use of an unreliable narrator who is a living demonstration of repression and self-repression. During the novel, he is slowly made to acknowledge what he had at first managed so successfully to hide from himself and to admit his culpability. But he still cannot be freed from his own conditioning; he is still a part of his society, and though he realises the truth he is powerless to act or to change the pre-set course of events. He must stand on the sidelines as Heidenreich, Kari's husband, commits suicide, his son goes to prison and Kari waits, alone and beyond his reach. He is the victim and the cause of the suffering.

Echoes of the enduring significance for Hoel of the fight against Fascism can be found in several of his later works, where it is again its relevance to Norwegian society which preoccupies him. In *Stevnemøte med glemte år* (1954), for example, he returns to the short-lived military resistance of 1940, to an investigation of how people reacted to the sudden attack. Some were heroic, but many were too cautious or too frightened – and when the heroes returned they were often treated with suspicion, as men who had deserted their jobs and run off, or as men with a secret love of violence. The war has become largely an excuse for the self-glorification of those who stayed behind – society has not grown more generous or more honest since the war, and the mechanism of social reaction, from which Nazism sprang, goes on as before. Circles are a favourite image of Hoel's, and the continuous cycle of repression is the most vicious circle of all.

The conscience of the writer: H. C. Branner and Martin A. Hansen

The image of the writer as a parasite on society is not infrequent in twentieth-century literature; and at times of social upheaval and violence the feeling of being a privileged observer, watching man's antics from a safe distance, is even more acute. This feeling is expressed most strongly in Scandinavian war literature by the Danish writers H. C. Branner and Martin A. Hansen, particularly in *Angst* and *Midsommerfesten*. In both of these *noveller* (short stories) the central character is the writer at work, trying to create literature out of the chaos and unable to avoid the knowledge that not only is he implicated in the general guilt but he must also bear a greater weight because he is using the suffering he sees around him as raw material for art, letting it inspire him and thus cynically profiting from it. The war has made him a moral criminal.

1. H. C. Branner (1903-66)

The theme of *angst* is a recurrent one in the works of H. C. Branner : man's fear at his own powerlessness, caught in a social machine which everyone else seems to understand better than he (*Legetøj*, 1936), fear of the marching feet which draw nearer and nearer (*Om lidt er vi borte*, 1939), and finally fear of the silent invader (the article 'Angst' in *Der brænder en Ild*, 1944). The two long *noveller Angst* (1947) and *Bjergene* (1953) – the latter set in the ruins of postwar Germany – represent a culmination of this theme. In *Angst* the writer tries to defend himself and his work first against his wife's accusations and then against his own conscience. His wife, a Jewess who has to flee for her own safety, taunts him with his inactivity – it is not he who risks his life ferrying refugees, his only fight is 'en Kamp med Ord som ingen har Brug for' (*'a fight with words that nobody needs'*) (p. 25). He tries to justify himself by saying that in his writing he is taking the sufferings of others upon himself:

> Det er ogsaa de andres Angst. . . . Jeg oplever det samme som de, bare paa en anden Maade. Jeg lider det samme. Og jeg føler noget som de slipper for at føle. Skammen over mig selv, Skammen ved at være Menneske. (p. 25)
>
> (*It's other people's fear too. . . . I experience the same as they do, only in a different way. I suffer the same thing. And I feel something they can avoid feeling. Ashamed of myself, ashamed of being human.*)

But he cannot convince himself or his wife, who tells him that he has subjected her, like everything else, to his words; their relationship has been nothing but a means for him to fend off the silence in which he would otherwise have to realise the truth. When she goes, he is indeed left in silence; but still he tries to ignore it and to convert his own fear and loneliness into literary capital. He projects it into the story he is writing about a condemned prisoner on his last night in his cell, and it becomes his inspiration.

But fortunately for himself he does not manage to repress his own feelings for long; he begins really to feel the fear of which he had previously talked. He panics when he cannot remember 'Ordet', the Word, which he thought he had found, and in desperation he turns to the Bible – to find the verse, quoted at the beginning of the *novelle*, in which Christ reproaches the sleeping disciples:

Og han kom og fandt dem sovende og sagde til Peter: Simon, sover du? Var du ikke i Stand til at vaage een Time?

(Mark 14,37)

(And he cometh, and findeth them sleeping, and saith unto Peter, Simon sleepest thou? couldest not thou watch one hour?)

He has lived in a half-sleep of words while his marriage crumbled and he let others fight for him. When he realises this, he becomes really frightened, to the extent of forgetting his own name; even that most familiar of words has become meaningless.

The second part of the *novelle* is a kind of dream-sequence in which the realities of the occupation are blended with the narrator's own mental disturbance. He tries continually to persuade himself that it is all a game really, that they are all children playing – such is the nightmare unreality of the occupation. But the only child in the story is a boy who sits in the street playing a drum, oblivious of the approaching danger until he is taken by the enemy. Like the writer he has carried on playing games for too long.

The writer goes out into the town, where in a grotesque puppet-like episode he watches – or imagines – the arrests, persecutions and murders carried out by the Gestapo and finally meets a girl in the crowd with whom he goes home. They go to bed together; but the sexual act, which elsewhere in Branner's writings can be a recalling to life and an affirmation of the healing power of human contact, means nothing at all. Afterwards, both are alone in the dark, as they were before. The curse of non-involvement has descended on the narrator; he cannot perform a meaningful act or reach out to another person.

As he walks home through the rain, the dawn comes and with it a faint glimpse of the possibility of coming alive again. The sound of marching feet has stopped; fear has gone, but there is nothing in its place. This is perhaps the beginning of a new courage which will enable him to face the consequences of his guilty conscience without trying to stifle it by insisting on the importance of his own role. But it is as yet only a glimpse – and one which is almost completely swallowed up again in the blackness. For the ending of the *novelle* is not the patch of blue sky but the writer back in his room, lying on his bed having reached, at last, the end of his words: 'jeg har ikke mere at sige' ('*I have no more to say*') (p. 63).

It seems a long way from Branner's first novel, *Legetøj*, which depicts the struggles of a little firm in an atmosphere of cut-throat competitiveness and quasi-Fascist reorganisation, to this account of the wanderings of a tormented mind. Yet there is a link between his early attacks on the inhumanity of the capitalist system which destroys the weakest and his preoccupation in later works with the role of the writer. The writer is part of the capitalist society and sells himself just as surely as the man who informs on his colleagues at work in return for a little extra money or prestige. Each is prepared to elbow his way up at the expense of his fellows and to take his talents to the highest bidder – a view which owes much to Branner's personal experience of working in a publicity firm and watching the authors coming in to beg for an advance, 'en evig værtshushistorie om gæld og spiritus og åndelig prostitution' ('*a never-ending sordid tale of debt and alcohol and spiritual prostitution*') (*Røde Heste i Sneen*, p. 17-18). In his play *Hundrede Kroner* (1949), Branner uses a writer as one example of the kind of people who are prepared to prostitute themselves for a little money; here is one who produces cheap pornography in order to earn enough to write his great novel which will reform society but never gets further than the pornography, cultivating his own bad conscience in the hope that one day it will be so bad that he will be forced to write:

> Jeg skammer mig dag og nat. Men daarlig samvittighed er kunstens stærkeste incitament. En dag sætter jeg mig hen og skriver min store sociale roman – i eet aandedrag. . . .
>
> (*Fem Radiospil*, p. 118)
>
> (*I feel ashamed of myself day and night. But a bad conscience provides the greatest impetus for art. One day I shall sit down and write my great social novel – all in one breath. . . .*)

In the same way the narrator in *Angst* clings to his own suffering, his own guilt as the very source of his inspiration. Perhaps a Kafka-like awareness of one's own involvement in the guilt of mankind is the nerve of the modern writer's condition; he is at once a victim of the system and a parasite living off it; this is his mark of Cain.

2. Martin A. Hansen (1909-55)

Cain was a familiar figure to Martin A. Hansen – and indeed a recurring one in his writings. Hansen's crisis of conscience during the war was concerned with an article – 'Dialog om Drab og Ansvar' (*Dialogue about Killing and Responsibility*) – which he wrote for *Der brænder en Ild*, a collection published by the underground press. In it he advocated the liquidation of informers. By speaking out in this way he maintained that he was as responsible for the death of these men as if he had actually killed them; it was an act that was to haunt him for the rest of his life. The burden that was laid upon him by this involvement in the violence of the Resistance, is evident from his letters and diaries. And there are clear traces of it too in his published work. The sustained joy of invention and comparative lightness of tone of his earlier novels, *Jonatans Rejse* (1941) and *Lykkelige Kristoffer* (1945), vanished for ever. From now on the mood was predominantly darker, and there was little evidence of story-telling for its own sake. Hansen had always felt uneasy about being a writer, leaving the family tradition of farming and following a path often regarded by those who labour with their hands as a disreputable one; but he was nevertheless able to conquer this feeling in his creative periods and produce works seemingly unaffected by his misgivings. By the end of the war, this feeling of guilt had taken on a more specific form. He knew that his words in 'Dialog om Drab og Ansvar' had inspired others to kill; the poet had become a murderer. His writing had made him feel that he stood outside the law of his own society.

Midsommerfesten is the longest of the three stories included in *Tornebusken* (1946), and although it is less directly concerned with war than the last of the three, *Septembertaagen*, which describes the rather pitiful military unpreparedness of Denmark in 1940, it clearly owes much to the time and the conditions of its composition. The story is on two levels; in an outer frame Forfatteren, the author, comments on his work under progress and talks to other people about it; interwoven with this are excerpts from the work itself. These two levels overlap at many points; the triangle Forfatteren – Læserinden (the lady reader) – Den syge Gud (the sick God) in the outer story is mirrored in the triangle in the inner story: Georg – Alma – Bedstefar (Grandfather). It is interesting to note that Forfatteren occupies the same position in his story as Georg does in his, for Georg is an emissary of the devil himself. There are several hints of similarity between the 'author' and his protagonist, especially in their feelings about the nature of the literary profession.

Much of the inspiration for this story came when Hansen was forced to go into hiding at the end of the war, and the circumstances of that time are much in evidence. The room in which Forfatteren is sitting is the guest-room in which Hansen was hiding at a friend's house, and it was actually while he was writing this that the friends with whom he had been working were arrested by the Nazis. So the situation Forfatteren describes to Læserinden is not invention but fact.

Forfatteren: De tænkte ikke et Øjeblik paa den Tid, jeg er i, og hvor nemt den kunde forhindre vort Samarbejde. Aldeles ikke. Det faldt Dem ikke ind, at nogle af mine Venner maaske kunde være blevet arresteret af Voldsmændene den Nat, vi to var

sammen. At de er i frygtelige Hænder nu. Det faldt Dem ikke
ind. Aldeles ikke.

Læserinden: Kan De da sidde her og fortælle Historier nu? De
maa da handle! Hvad vil De gøre?

Forfatteren: Hvad der er at gøre.

(p. 163)

(The author: *It didn't occur to you for a moment to think about the
time I'm living in, and how easily it could interrupt our work together.
Not at all it didn't. It never crossed your mind that some of my friends
could perhaps have been arrested by men of violence the night we two
were together. That they are in fearful hands now. It never crossed
your mind. Not at all.*

The lady reader: *But how can you sit here and tell stories now? You
must do something! What are you going to do?*

The author: *What there is to do.*)

And 'what there is to do' is to continue with the story. The author
cannot do anything for those he knows are now suffering – all he can
do is just carry on writing in the knowledge that this is not helping
them at all. Meanwhile, the double pressure of guilt at having avoided
the same torments and haste, for perhaps he does not have much time
left himself, has so inspired him that he must write. He sees himself as
a betrayer, uses the image of Pilate – 'Jeg trænger til at vaske Hænder.
Der hænger Blæk og andet ved' ('*I must wash my hands. They're stained
with ink and other things*') (p. 118) – but keeps on writing. The image of
Cain is of course not far from his mind either. Asked by Den syge
Gud, 'Cain, where is your brother?', he replies as did Cain: 'Am I my
brother's keeper?':

> Hvorfor skal jeg se alle de Genfærd og Skikkelser her? . . . Har
> jeg lille Dværg da ikke siddet uskyldigt her og passet mit for-
> dømte Arbejde? Er jeg da den skyldige?
>
> (p. 162)
>
> (*Why must I see all these ghosts and apparitions here? . . . Haven't I,
> little dwarf that I am, been sitting here innocently getting on with my
> damned work? Am I the guilty one?*)

He tries in vain to reason away his guilt; he is guilty almost by
definition as a writer. It is not fortuitous that Georg in the inner story
compares an author to a criminal; for Martin A. Hansen, fictional
writing is akin to a criminal activity or at the very least is morally
reprehensible:

> man kan jo være uklar og kejtet i Begyndelsen, naar man prøver
> sig frem. Men den fri Forbryder kan udvikle sig, ligesom en god

Skribent, hvis første Forsøg har været tvivlsomme.

(p. 215)

(You can be a bit unsure and clumsy to start with, when you're still experimenting. But a free criminal can get better at it, just like a good writer whose first efforts were rather shaky.)

Georg defends himself vigorously against the suggestion that he is a failed writer who has gone over to 'en anden Tyvenæring' (*'another dishonest way of earning a living'*) (p. 216) – he regards it as a substitute for living. Not everything Georg says can be taken as having Martin A. Hansen's approval; but these words must have lain close to what he was thinking at the time and are in the same spirit as his remarks about his planned work *Kains Alter*: 'Digteren er en Livssynder' (*'to be a writer is to be a sinner'*) (Th. Bjørnvig: *Kains Alter*, p. 270).

The immediate impact of the war on both Hansen and Branner was that they saw it not only as a crisis for their society but as a crisis for themselves as writers. Thus it is not only a preoccupation of their writings; it affects the very way in which they write. The straightforward narrative account of *Legetøj* and the carefully balanced construction of *Lykkelige Kristoffer* are abandoned for a fragmentary technique, which in *Angst* becomes almost a stream of consciousness and in *Midsommerfesten* a jerky alternation between scraps of dialogue and excerpts from the 'story'. Both works contain passages in which normal reality breaks down, dreamlike sequences in which a logical progression of events gives way to a fairytale happening, as when Georg starts to fly, or to a grotesque and obscene ritual, as when the writer in *Angst* observes the arrest of a suspect. The writer's neurosis is mirrored in the incoherence of a style which formerly was for both authors more controlled and consistent; it is a world of uncertainty in which anything may happen.

The sense of being invaded by an enemy, of being out of control and not knowing one's place any longer in a society which has lost its bearings, is strong in both of these *noveller*. The central characters are outside normal society, cut off by their own situation – both have for various reasons been forced into hiding and therefore into isolation. The books take place in a kind of limbo, out of the real world and out of time; the writers are unable to influence what they know is happening around them. They are marooned in the centre of life, condemned merely to sit and observe – and relate. Their surroundings are a physical expression of their place outside the mainstream of existence.

Chapter Two

Sweden: The 'Sixties

The chapter-headings in Torben Brostrøm's *Moderne svensk litteratur* (1973) give a rough indication of the central literary preoccupations of the last three decades in Sweden. The three sections are entitled *Verdenskrig og 40-tal* (*The World War and the 1940s*), *Modernisme og 50-tal* (*Modernism and the 1950s*) and *Politisk Bevidsthed og 60-tal* (*Political Awareness and the 1960s*). Brostrøm subscribes to the view held by the majority of literary critics – that the literature of the 1960s owes a great deal to that of the 1940s. The wartime years produced what is commonly referred to as 'beredskapsdiktning' ('literature of readiness'. This specifically Swedish term refers to the literature produced by writers of a neutral country who tried in their writings to make some contribution, to take part, mentally at least, in the battle.) They were followed by a reaction, an involvement with the internal problems of form and aesthetics. In recent years, however, the word 'beredskap' has once more been widely used, this time in a somewhat more aggressive sense.

> Det är på flera sätt motiverat att jämföra vårt decennium med 40-talet, och det har också gjorts. Här ser vi en punkt där de markant skiljer sig åt: ingen talar om ångest, ingen om vårt behov av tröst. I stället syns som sagt ett slags beredskapsanda, en som om-hållning: frågan om vi är maktlösa är i grunden oviktig, det viktiga är att leva *som om* vi inte vore det.
>
> (*29 röster-67*, p. 32)
>
> (*Our decade is in many ways reminiscent of the 1940s, and the comparison has been made before. Yet in one aspect the two are markedly different: no one now speaks of fear, no one speaks of our need to be consoled. Instead we find, as I have indicated, a kind of spirit of readiness, an attitude of defiance: the question as to whether we are powerless or not is basically an unimportant one. The important thing is to live as if we were not.*)

This summary of developments during the past thirty years is of course schematic. Yet to describe the 1960s as a period when Swedish writers as a whole became more politically orientated is not to make too sweeping a statement; even those who tried not to let politics intrude into their writing in any way felt the need to explain their position, to justify their refusal to participate in what they recognised was the mood of the age. The reasons for this 'politicisation of literature' are manifold, for, in contrast with the 1940s, there was no sudden catastrophe which demanded an immediate response. It was partly a reaction against what was seen as an obsession with the formal aspect of literature in the 1950s (a reaction expressed in the 1960 manifesto *Front mot formens tyranni*, by Sonja Åkesson and others) and a general desire for a more committed kind of writing. Knowledge about the problems of the Third World and their causes was also gradually spreading (Franz Fanon's *Les Damnés de la Terre* was published in Swedish in 1962) and there was a growing disillusion with Sweden itself, both with its attitude towards developing countries and with its treatment of its own citizens. It was in the latter half of the 1960s that these concerns came to a head.

A further impulse towards commitment, and the single most important catalyst in the formation of the radical protest, was the war in Vietnam. It was this conflict above all others which brought to a climax the uneasy stirrings of bad conscience in writers who were becoming aware that in Sweden's case neutrality in fact implied tacit consent to war-mongering and economic profiteering at the expense of those who were already poor. Göran Sonnevi's poem 'Om kriget i Vietnam' (1965) is perhaps the best-known literary comment and was one of the starting-points of the debate. Like many writers after him, he contrasted his own experiences of Vietnam – TV pictures of hunted Viet-Cong and interviews with cheerful American fighter pilots – with his Swedish reality.

> Här dör knappast någon
> av annat än personliga skäl. Den svenska
> ekonomin dödar numera
> inte många, i varje fall
> inte här i landet.

(Det gäller oss, p. 110)

> *(Here hardly anybody dies*
> *for other reasons than purely personal ones. The Swedish*
> *economy doesn't kill*
> *many any more, at least*
> *not in this country.)*

The belief that it is impossible to avoid responsibility for what is happening in other parts of the world was forcefully expressed by many writers and was dependent on and reinforced a realisation of the injustices inherent in the democratic system at home. This resulted not only in a shift in what was regarded as the proper subject of literature but also in a widening of the author's view of his role in society. Many more authors are now journalists, critics, debators, TV personalities; they travel around the country spreading and gathering information, take part in demonstrations, visit schools to talk directly with the young. Författarcentrum (*The Authors' Centre*), started in 1967, is one expression of the general desire of many authors to make personal contact with their public, rather than to rely solely on the medium of books. Indeed, so free is their access through many channels to their audience that some writers have become aware of a new danger, that of excessive tolerance; they are not taken seriously enough for any restraints on their activities to be considered necessary, and thus they are effectively rendered harmless.

The demand for an actively committed literature has been met in a variety of ways. At one extreme are writers such as the poet Bengt Emil Johnson who refuse to convey any message at all, preferring to experiment with the shapes and sounds of words, their musical and graphic qualities; although Johnson himself maintains that precisely such attempts to create a new way of communicating are necessary before a new consciousness can be created. If the traditional forms are used, with all their contaminations, 'belastade med ett hävdvunnet innehåll av gamla värderingar' ('*burdened with all the time-honoured weight of ancient value judgments*') (*29 röster-67*, p. 72), one cannot hope to convey a new way of looking at the world. But if, indeed, man's thinking can be changed in this way, it will be a long, slow process – and as yet there is no evidence that this restructuring of language has had any practical consequences for the governing of society.

Torsten Ekbom is another writer whose works seem politically irrelevant. The emphasis in his novels is also on experimentation, on breaking away from the traditional genre to try new methods of composition; at times the result seems like mystification, at times like an absorbing interest in creating abstract patterns. Yet, as is made clear in his contribution to the collection of interviews in *27 röster-67*, Ekbom is far from being politically indifferent or unaware. He does not believe his work exists in a vacuum and has often stated his disagreement with what he sees as the oversimplified modern distinction between aesthetics and politics in literature. He does not find any opposition between aestheticism and commitment but believes that they can reinforce each other; he has come nearest to achieving this in *En galakväll på Operan* (1969), a work which brings together in seemingly random fashion operatic scenarios, discussion of scientific experiments, scenes from everyday life, accounts of competitions, lists of objects– and yet which gradually forms itself into a demonstration of a progression, of the development of modern society through advances in technology and practical psychology, culminating in the total manipulation of its members.

Though sensitivity to current ideas can be traced in the works of writers such as Johnson and Ekbom, neither of them is a polemicist attempting to influence the immediate actions of society or to comment on a particular series of events. They are both 'difficult' writers, addressing a cultural elite, and it is only through a process of gradual dissemination that they can have any effect on non-literary circles. At the other end of the literary spectrum are those who have become convinced of the need to speak out directly in their writings– and have sometimes felt it so urgently that they have abandoned creative literature in favour of forms of writing which might reach a wider audience than the literary one. From a standpoint outside party politics (unlike that of some of the more 'moderate' authors, such as Per Olov Enquist, who remain within the framework of the Social-Democratic party), they attack the basic principles of Swedish democracy. I shall look more closely at the writings of Jan Myrdal and Sara Lidman, later on; another important figure is Göran Palm, who began writing as a poet and who later published factual, often statistical, studies of the plundering of the Third World by the West (*En orättvis betraktelse*, 1966) and the indoctrination to which 'democratic' countries subject their members (*Indoktrineringen i Sverige*, 1968). He still continues to publish poetry; unlike Jan Myrdal, he believes that the possession of literary facility adds to the possibilities of reaching an audience. Yet his principal influence as a writer undoubtedly derives from his factual writings, in which he can use his poet's sensitivity to words and their meanings as a fine instrument, to detect hidden prejudice and subterfuge.

Between these two extremes are many authors whose work bears evidence of their political involvement but who have remained primarily literary figures. Sven Delblanc's *Nattresa* (1967) and *Åsnebrygga* (1969) portray, the former in novel and the latter in diary form, his realisation of the need to humanise Western society; P. C. Jersild, in *Grisjakten* (1968) and *Vi ses i Song My* (1970) studies the power of the bureaucracy over the minds of its members and its facility for accommodating those who try to reform it. The poet Björn Håkanson, always a social critic, turned specifically to the Vietnam conflict in *Kärlek i Vita Huset* (1967) and to the Swedish political situation in *Mellan två val* (1969). Sven Lindqvist's *Myten om Wu Tao-tzu* (1967), Staffan Beckman's *Tycker du att George är en galning* (1968) and many more are part of the same trend. Per Olov Enquist

35

and Göran Sonnevi, whom I shall discuss shortly, also belong in this category.

In a discussion of the various forms of political literature in Sweden, it is useful to recall the distinction drawn (with reference to the novel) between the documentary form and the document by Göran Printz-Påhlson in his essay 'Norman Mailer och det dokumentariska' (*Slutna världar öppen rymd*, pp. 242-3.) He represents this distinction by means of a diagram in which the horizontal axis tends towards greater realism (i.e. verisimilitude) and the vertical towards greater truth (i.e. verifiable fact).

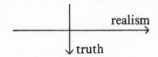

Fiction thus belongs above the horizontal axis, historical accounts below it. That fiction which is furthest from the semblance of reality, the romantic tale, is placed to the left of the vertical axis and that which appears closer to reality, the documentary novel, to the right. Similarly, the historical account which has a low claim to credibility, the historical novel, occupies the place to the left below the line, and on the right goes the document, which approaches most nearly to both actual fact and verisimilitude.

fiction:	romantic tale		documentary novel
history:	historical novel		document

It is the literature to the right of the vertical axis with which I am concerned now. The documentary novel is a form much used by modern Swedish writers such as Per Olof Sundman and Per Olov Enquist, whose *Legionärerna* is a good example. Finally I shall look at various attempts to approach closer to an undistorted presentation of the facts than the novel allows – though if one agrees with Printz-Påhlson's proviso that the document 'gäller oberoende av sin upphovsman' ('*exists independently of its writer*') (*Slutna världar öppen rymd*, p. 243), one cannot– or at least, one cannot yet– accept that any of these attempts do come that close, since the personality of the writer, especially when he is well-known and authoritative as are those whom I shall examine, is inevitably part of the work: it is impossible to dissociate the name and its connotations from the facts presented, and therefore one is bound to see them in a somewhat different light.

Literature as a vehicle for commitment: Per Olov Enquist and Göran Sonnevi

1. Per Olov Enquist (1934-)

A desire to give his novels a firm basis of historical documentation has always been apparent in the work of Per Olov Enquist. In *Magnetisörens femte vinter* (1964), which is based on the life of the hypnotist Anton Mesmer, the documentation remains in the background; the only reference to actual sources is in a brief note at the end of the book, and the use of the diary form and the references to contemporary accounts are a fictional device employed expressly to increase the appearance of authenticity. This is a historical novel springing from research rather than an account of the research itself. Enquist's next novel, *Hess* (1966), is very different. Ostensibly written by a narrator who is researching into Rudolf Hess' manuscripts, it develops into anything but the methodic, painstaking amassing of evidence that one would expect. In seemingly random fashion, the book combines notes on research, the narrator's personal memories, literary pastiches, imaginative reconstructions of various roles. Here too, history is used very freely, but the result is not a novel with a historical background but an account of the meeting between historical fact and the mind of the author, which explores the mind rather than the fact.

In *Legionärerna* (1968), the meeting is again between historical fact and the mind of the author, but this time there is a determined attempt to let fact dominate, the author merely co-ordinating the evidence. The problem of how to achieve this, if one can – or should – becomes the centre of the novel. The object of the research in this book is the highly fraught debate which happened in Sweden at the end of the Second World War about the fate of the refugees from the Baltic states who had sought safety in the country. Enquist looks at the contemporary documents, visits the places where the action happened, talks to those still alive who participated, even goes to Latvia to find some of the former refugees – and records in meticulous detail each step of his investigation of the events which led to the final decision to send the Balts home. Yet he is made constantly aware, and reminds the reader continuously, of his own presence as selector and compiler of material and of the fact that he cannot refrain from expressing some comment on his theme in the very way he presents it. He soon abandons all attempt to give an 'objective' account; he draws attention to his own methods, casts suspicion on his choice of facts, demonstrates how he puts an interpretation on statistics which favours the left-wing viewpoint and puts the blame on the Swedes for creating hysteria about Russian brutality. The book is at once an attempt at impartiality and a demonstration of the author's involvement.

For Enquist is not, as he makes clear in the course of the book, merely a disinterested reader elucidating the facts of a vanished age. He has been led to his subject by a personal search for commitment which took him first to the freedom marches in Jackson, Mississippi, in 1966, a cause which he tried, but found impossible, to make his own. He remained an outsider, unable to experience the solidarity he saw all around. And it is suggested that this is a specifically Swedish experience, to be a neutral observer of other people's conflicts: 'Svenskarna har världens enda transportabla samveten, de åker runt som professionella moralister' ('*Swedes possess the world's only portable consciences, they travel around as professional moralists*') (p. 29). But of course Sweden is not without conflicts, and the friend who criticised the portable consciences of the Swedes soon shows Enquist where to look for one that concerns him more nearly. One of the most testing situations in which Sweden recently found itself was the Second World War; then, too, there was a growing sense of bad conscience, at being apart from the suffering and even refusing to help. The latent guilt feelings were whipped up into a frenzy of emotion at the prospect of the Balts' return home.

So the novel becomes a study of the growth of a cause, of the way in which the determination to leave a position of neutrality and find solidarity in working for a common end can lead to an overhasty commitment, of the need to examine one's own motives and not to think that any action is a good action. It is also an exposé of the functioning of the democratic machine, of the haphazard way in which decisions are reached, and criticises the awe in which most people hold their elected rulers, for 'politik var inte förbehållen någon' ('*politics are not the special preserve of anyone*'). Above all, however, it is a personal account of the author's failure simply to present what happened, not only because of the author's own motives but also because *the* truth about the past simply does not exist.

> Situationen kan inte beskrivas i sin helhet, den kan inte behandlas objektivt, möjligtvis sakligt, och den förändras oupphörligt, beroende på hur man vill använda den. Den här boken handlar om ett utsnitt av baltutlämningen, åren 1945-1968.
> (p. 9)
>
> (*The situation cannot be described in its entirety, it cannot be treated objectively; the most one can do is to base one's account on facts. And it changes constantly, depending on how one wishes to use it. This*

book deals with an excerpt of the repatriation of the Balts, the years 1945-68.)

Enquist himself calls his work a novel, in the knowledge that he has told one of the possible stories about what happened. He has not succeeded in crossing the line which divides the novel from the factual account. Complete objectivity cannot of course be attained, but he has renounced the attempt to adopt even the impersonal role of the historian. The story of the Balts becomes as it were internalised, an image of his own struggle between the desire to see both sides of an issue, which precludes joining either side, and the need to take part in the action, which involves surrendering a balanced view and deliberately choosing one-sidedness. Clearly his sympathies in his writing do tend towards the left, and the effect of his investigation is to redress the balance somewhat in favour of the Russians; but he remains aware that these sympathies may prejudice a full understanding of the situation. It is perhaps the ultimate dilemma of the intellectual in politics.

2. Göran Sonnevi (1939-)

The poet Göran Sonnevi is also continually conscious in his work of his own presence and its relation to what he is looking at. When asked what he considered to be his role in society as a writer, he replied: 'Att artikulera tankar och känslor inför den del av det totala skeendet som det är möjligt för mig att omfatta' (*'to give expression to thoughts and feelings within that part of the total course of events which it is possible for me to grasp'*) (*29 röster-67*, p. 89). And it is *his* experience of the world which is communicated, as I have already pointed out in reference to his poem 'Om kriget i Vietnam', which describes a Swedish view of the war rather than trying to postulate the thoughts and emotions of a Viet-Cong.

The Vietnam poem is included in the collection *ingrepp-modeller* (1965), which made Sonnevi well-known as a poet. His two earlier collections, *Outfört* (1961) and *Abstrakta dikter* (1963), contain on the whole more private, personal poems. In his later works (*och nu!*, 1967; *Det måste gå*, 1970; *Det oavslutade språket*, 1972) the commitment becomes more insistent. His poetry registers the main international events of those years, with clear disapproval of the imperialist wielders of military power; his sympathies lie with the poor and oppressed. Yet he does not react simply in political terms; the answer is not to be found only in the redistribution of wealth and power. Sonnevi shares with poets such as Bengt Emil Johnson the feeling that the very

39

language at his disposal is contaminated, that a new language, a new structure must be discovered before the old prejudices can be conquered. But, unlike the concrete poets, he chooses to use the language as it is, with all its imperfections, in order to speak directly of the need to renew it, to learn the language of the as yet unborn child, the only one which corruption has not yet reached.

> Det ropar på ett språk som inte kan finnas
> Det ropar med
> de nakna kompetenserna till språk. . . .
> Om barnet föds får vi lära oss
> tala den oföddes språk.
> ('Den oföddes språk', from *Det måste gå*, p. 68-9).
> (*'It cries out in a language which cannot exist*
> *It cries out with*
> *the bare possibilities of language. . . .*
> *If the child is born we must learn*
> *to speak the language of the unborn.*)

Images of unborn children in the womb, of birth and of the newly born are frequent in Sonnevi's poetry. As well as the political poems there are many which are personal, even private, expressing warm affection and closeness to his beloved and tenderness towards the child he has created within her. Concern with world affairs never wholly excludes the gentler, more intimate moments of life – though it may intrude into them and is a constant threat to their existence, as in the poem just quoted, in which the unborn child is defenceless against man's brutality.

> Det biologiska och kemiska kriget
> bränner ner
> den oavslutade hjärnan
> (*The biological and chemical war*
> *burns up*
> *the unfinished brain*)

The poet is conscious of living in a privileged society, and even in his most carefree moments he cannot forget that in most of the world children are born with no chance at all. It seems almost beyond the bounds of possibility that something can happen to change all this.

And yet hope has not entirely vanished. This very preoccupation in Sonnevi's poetry with beginnings – new language, new life – will not allow him to tolerate such defeatism. Although the chances may be getting slimmer, still each new child represents fresh possibilities; time is running out, but it is not yet too late to stop the cycle of destruction.

Språket väntar på
att få bryta sig ut ur ditt liv och
förändra världen
Hur mycket tid finns det kvar?
Vita, språklösa
gener ger nu världen dess form!
Den möjliga
kärlekens språk nu måste tala
med vapen!

(Det gäller oss, p. 153-4)

(Language is waiting
to break out of your body and
change the world
How much time is left?
White, speechless
Genes are now giving form to the world!
The potential
language of love must now speak
with weapons!)

For Sonnevi, 'vit' (white) is one of the most contaminated words in the language; far from indicating freshness and purity, it carries for him connotations of the oppression of the white man's rule, the white smoke of American bombs, the cold sterility of scientific advance, bereft of human warmth, the destruction of life for which he too is responsible, for 'vi har vitmenat globen' ('*we have whitewashed the earth*') (Det gäller oss, p. 123).

His own leisure to enjoy the warmth of family life depends, he realises, on the continued exploitation of the rest of the globe; he cannot enjoy it without guilt when he knows what is happening. He is compelled to work for the destruction of the present system, to believe in its destruction. There will be no miraculous revolution: the change must be wrought by those who are themselves already implicated in the guilt of society, already far removed from their original potential. One can never make an entirely fresh start, as the world cannot be new again.

Då är det kanske bättre att
göra nytt alltsammans?
Det är klart
Men det finns bara dom här
människorna som
finns här,
slitna, förbrukade   Och det måste gå

41

För det går ju
inte utan människor
Även om dom flesta inte fungerar så bra
är dom inte skit
Vi är inte skit
('Det är svårt att reparera', from *Det gäller oss*, p. 159)
(So perhaps it would be better to
start from scratch again?
Certainly it would
But there are only these
people who
are here
worn out, exhausted   *But it's got to work*
Because it won't work
without people
Even if most of them don't function too well
they're not rubbish
We're not rubbish)

'Det måste gå' – the tone is half pleading, half commanding. The twin images of birth and contamination in Sonnevi's poetry embody his hope that out of the old and corrupt society a new one may one day emerge.

The inadequacy of literature: Jan Myrdal and Sara Lidman

1. Jan Myrdal (1927-   )

Jan Myrdal is one of the dominant figures in contemporary Swedish culture and cannot be ignored in any account of the political trends in literature in recent years. The books he wrote in the 1950s are less well known, though they deserve some attention for what they reveal both of the themes which run throughout his work and of the development in thought which led to a change in his mode of expression. In those early years, he was a fictional writer, a creator of comic and fantastic tales with a love of the absurd and the grotesque, almost Rabelaisian in his broad humour. *Jubelvår* (1955) describes the wild orgies and dramatic clashes in a provincial Swedish town, Ljungsvik, on the occasion of its seven hundredth anniversary celebrations. *Badrumskranen* (1957) weaves an involved plot full of exaggeration and coincidence around an ornamental bath-tap, whose adventures radically change the lives of several people. There is no dearth of inventiveness or wit in the author's imagination; and yet the stories are more than just excuses for its indulgence. The role of the writer *vis-à-vis* his creation is considered within the novels themselves. In *Jubelvår* the central character is the author who is writing the story; he has a certain control over events but loses that control when he loses his manuscript and falls into the power of his invented characters. His autonomy is very insecure. In *Badrumskranen* the author remains more in the background but occasionally draws the reader's attention in a half-mocking way to the gratuitous absurdity of his labours; he is only writing a 'leksaksberättelse', a light entertainment, which cannot be allowed to become too serious or too tragic. And one of the characters in this novel is an author himself, who sits and writes romantic stories while dreaming of writing something which would show people what their lives were really like and how they could change them. The strength of Myrdal's own desire to show people what their lives are really like is evident in these novels too, especially in *Jubelvår*, in which the frivolity is suddenly forgotten in a Kafkaesque vision of man's powerlessness in the grip of the social machine, as in the description of the irreversibility of the judicial process, even when the wrong man is on trial. Ljungsvik bears a close resemblance to the Swedish society Myrdal attacks in his later books.

> Ljungsvik låg i ett demokratiskt land. Det låg faktiskt i världens mest demokratiska land. Ty innevånarna hade de mest vidsträckta fri- och rättigheter, som exempelvis att tro på vilka vallöften de ville, att hylla vilken fotbollsstjärna de ville, att föräl ska sig i vilken filmstjärna de kunde, att äga hur mycket pengar som helst och ta vilket arbete som bjöds dem.
>
> (pp. 80-1)

> (*Ljungsvik was in a democratic country. In fact it was in the world's most democratic country. For the inhabitants had the most far-reaching rights and freedoms, for example to believe in whichever election promises they chose, to support any football star they wanted, to fall in love with any film star they fancied, to own as much money as they liked and take the work that was offered them.*)

Since 1960, Myrdal has written hardly any fiction; he took the consequences of his realisation that the function of the fictional author has always been to lull his readers into comfortable unawareness of the actual conditions of their lives and decided that any novel he might write, however good, would serve only to conceal the truth.

> Det vore lögn det hela. Läsarna kunde lika gärna röka hasch. . . .
> När pendlaren pendlat färdigt läser han pendlarromaner. Så går

hans liv. Om inte även trälar och trälars barn lyssnat till Njals saga så hade de kunnat resa sig ur lorten.

(Skriftställning, p. 212)
(It would be a lie from beginning to end. The readers might as well smoke hash. . . . When a commuter has finished commuting he reads commuter-novels. That's how his life goes. If slaves and the children of slaves had not listened to Njal's Saga they would have been able to raise themselves from the dirt.)

Myrdal has become a journalist and reporter, trying by every means at his disposal to communicate his arguments to his public. He has travelled widely and has published reports of other societies, particularly those very different from his own; of these *Rapport från kinesisk by* (1963) *(Report from a Chinese Village)* is the most widely read. He has written a semi-autobiographical account of the position of the intellectual in modern society *(Samtida bekännelser av en europeisk intellektuell*, 1964), playlets with a moral for everyman *(Moraliteter*, 1967) and many articles in the daily press (collected in several volumes entitled *Skriftställning* of which the first was published in 1968.),

In the preface to the first volume of *Skriftställning*, Myrdal drew attention to what he believed to be three decisive dates in his life: '1954 (när jag debuterade), 1958 (när jag kom till revolutionernas Asien), 1963 (när jag återvände till Sverige)' *('1954 (when I made my literary debut), 1958 (when I arrived in revolutionary Asia), 1963 (when I returned to Sweden')*, (p. 6). I have already considered the first phase of his writing; the second reached its fullest expression in *Rapport från kinesisk by*. First-hand experience of conditions in the poorer countries of the world brought home to him the real economic basis of Swedish prosperity, and he directed his efforts to opening his countrymen's eyes to injustice on a global scale and to describing the possibilities for change as they were being realised elsewhere, particularly in China. *Rapport från kinesisk by* is an attempt to give an unbiased documentary account of what is happening in the new China as it is seen by those who are participating in its development, a record of interviews with the inhabitants of a country village. In his preface he anticipates the objections which might be raised about the reliability of his report: the artificiality of the interview form, the awe in which he was held as a distinguished foreign visitor, the added possibilities for error or misunderstanding involved in the use of an interpreter, the danger of faulty memory in even the most co-operative talker, the inevitability of some personal involvement on his part which might distort the evidence presented. But his awareness of these dangers and his conscious efforts to reduce the margin of error produced a work which seems to be as accurate an account of Chinese reality in the early 1960s as it was possible for a Westerner to give – an edited document. At the same time, its place in Myrdal's works gives the report a significance which perhaps it might otherwise not have had; it becomes a demonstration of a decentralised society striving towards social equality and invites comparison with the highly centralised, class-ridden social systems of the Western world.

On his return to Sweden in 1963, Myrdal viewed his country with the fresh eyes of someone who has been absent for a while; and he soon became convinced that the inequality of Swedish society was growing (v. *Fallet Sverige, marginalanteckningar*, from *Clarté* Nr.2, 1963). He now focused on his own country's problems, seeing them however in a global perspective and himself as a European who shares the common guilt of a comfortable cultural elite occupied with aesthetic puzzles while the world perishes around them (v. *Samtida*). The tone in Myrdal's later works, however, is more often one of accusation than of confession; his investigation of other communities had made more glaring the faults at home, and his belief that things were getting rapidly worse gave him a sense of urgency which made him turn all his energies to making others aware of the crisis. Much of his recent writing conveys an impression of obsessive haste; he has no time for friends, for family, for illness – he is impatient of anything which detracts from his self-appointed task. Any story-telling in which he indulges is never for its own sake, and he represses any material extraneous to the message – as in *Moraliteter* (1967), where the point is hammered relentlessly home in a series of 'trials' which find the central characters guilty of petty-bourgeois conformity, cowardice and opportunism. His experiences have brought him to the point at which he sees the professedly unpolitical author as a fool or a hypocrite; literature cannot but be a political act.

Diskussionerna om engagemang och politisk litteratur finner jag meningslösa. Lika meningslösa som esteternas tal om 'konst'. Om man vet att det skrivna skrivs för läsare och om man vet hur man själv förändrats av lästa ord då bör man inse att skrivandet är en social (och därmed) politisk handling oavsett vad skrivaren själv tror eller inte tror; den förnuftige handlar medvetet.

(*Svenska Dagbladet* 5/2/67)

(*Discussions about commitment and political literature I find meaningless. Just as meaningless as the aesthete's speeches about 'art'. If you know that what is written is written in order to be read, and if you know how you yourself are changed by the words you read, then you must realise that writing is a social (and therefore) political activity,*

45

*regardless of what the writer himself believes or does not believe; the
man of sense takes the consequences of this.)*

2. Sara Lidman (1923-   )

Sara Lidman's development as a writer has been quite similar to
that of Jan Myrdal, beginning in the 1950s with novels and moving
away from fiction during the 1960s. And for her, too, the experience
of a foreign culture and its differences from her own was a decisive
factor in the change of direction. Her first four novels are set in her
native Västerbotten, in north-east Sweden, and portray Swedish provincial society.

Then, after a visit to South Africa in 1960-1, came two novels, *Jag
och min son* (1961) and *Med fem diamanter* (1964), which bear witness
to the shock of witnessing apartheid and exploitation. *Jag och min son*
describes the society of Johannesburg as seen through the eyes of a
would-be white colonialist who has failed to make money even in a
place where it is so easy to make and pours all his frustrations into an
obsessive love for his son, the four-year-old Igor, who clings to the
generous warmth of his black nanny and gradually rejects his father's
hysterical demands for proof of affection. This trio, set against the
latent and repressed violence of the town as a whole, with its black
slums and white villas, act out the clash between two ways of life, the
grasping, self-centred European and the spontaneous 'here and now'
attitude of the African. *Med fem diamanter* takes place in Kenya, and
again it is the frictions between black and white which form the
background to the story of an individual, the young African Wachira,
who struggles in vain for the right to support his wife and family and
still see them from time to time. Working as a 'boy' with a white
family, he is expected to lie and steal, and he is humiliated and cheated
until he turns, in his rage, on his own brother. In this society, an
African can become successful only by himself becoming an exploiter
of his fellow men.

The indignation Sara Lidman felt at the social injustice she saw in
Africa is clearly evident in these stories. Yet they are still novels;
although the factual basis is apparent to the reader, one becomes
involved in the individual characters rather than being drawn in the
first instance to a consideration of the evils of the society. Sara Lidman
must have felt that fiction was at best an indirect appeal to action, for
in her subsequent works she spoke out more directly in her own
person.

Samtal i Hanoi (1966) is an autobiographical account of a visit to Vietnam in 1965 and records the writer's observations and her numerous interviews, with both Vietnamese and outsiders like herself. The tone throughout the book is emotional, an unreserved admiration of the Vietnamese and anger and shame at the aggressors, to whom, by virtue of her origin, she belongs. Here at last is a people which refuses to accept the myth of the white man's superiority, of the capitalist's inalienable right to take what he wants and leave the scrapings for those to whom the land should belong. The description of this little people taking on the Goliath of America becomes lyrical, almost a hymn to their unassuming courage and matter-of-fact cheerfulness in the face of what seem impossible odds. The book opens with a description of the approach to Vietnam by train, in which the sentences are often short, precise and factual, but at the same time full of romantic imagery. The train itself is personified as a steadfast plodder, which 'sätter en ära i att klara backarna utan att behöva be passagerarna skjuta på' (*'makes it a point of honour to get up the slopes without having to ask the passengers to get out and push'*) (p. 9); the calm scene is lit by a moon which is 'drypande blank som om den just stigit upp ur en varm smorning' (*'shiny and dripping, as if it had just been anointed with warm oil'*) (p. 7), and the Vietnamese passengers seem like men from an earlier age, 'gossar som de var i begynnelsen' (*'lads just as they were in the beginning'*) (p. 7).

And so the book continues, alternating between indignation and identification; it is not an attempt to elucidate the facts impartially but a declaration of faith, a conscious political act. In an introduction written later the author admits that the work was a first unsure step on a new path and recognises its unevenness; but she reiterates her hope that such writing will not merely provide an aesthetic experience for the reader but will incite him to action. The legacy of her earlier writing is apparent in the style, and in this way the book is not entirely removed from her novels; one feels the presence of Sara Lidman the author, creating sympathy for the Vietnamese as for Africans by a turn of phrase, a carefully-placed detail. Like Enquist's *Legionärerna*, it is an account of the meeting between a trained awareness and a historical situation; but Sara Lidman is conscious before she begins of exactly where she stands, and thus she attempts to engage the reader's sympathies for the events themselves and not for any internal conflicts, as Enquist does. Yet the effect of the highly coloured style runs somewhat counter to her intention, directing the reader's attention back towards the personality of the author.

The critics remarked on the emotional tone of *Samtal i Hanoi* when the book appeared, and the negative criticism had its effect on Sara

Lidman. In her next book, *Gruva* (1968), she returned to a Swedish setting, with vision sharpened, like Jan Myrdal's, by an insight into other forms of society. The book is a report on the mining community in Svappavaara and is based on a series of interviews which she recorded herself. The lesson of *Samtal i Hanoi* is not forgotten; there is very little direct comment by the author. The miners are allowed to speak for themselves, and it is largely in their words that the story of their lives is told. Sara Lidman is careful to account for her methods and to emphasise the ability of the miners to articulate their problems themselves; she stresses how little editing was required. Yet there is more in the book than the words of the miners, and it is in the choice and placing of other passages that her own involvement in the strife becomes apparent. The scene is not simply surveyed impartially; Sara Lidman's writing is always a contribution to a debate, even here where she refrains from making a speech herself. One must read the whole text in the light of the introductory chapter, which gives a clearly sympathetic glimpse into the *milieu* of the workers and sets up as motto and anti-motto two quotations, one by Fanon which argues that technological advance can only be of advantage to a society which is organically ready to accept it, and the other by the director of the mines which maintains that technical questions can be decided by experts alone and cannot be a matter for democratic discussion. And there are no interviews with the employers; the other side is represented by jargon from time-and-motion studies and impersonal official documents, clearly intended to form a jarring contrast with the colloquial dialogue of the workers. This does not necessarily make the picture presented any less true, but it does indicate so obvious a bias that the suspicions of a wary reader might be awakened, making him a little reluctant to accept such passages as evidence.

This objection apart, the contrast between the two modes of expression does point to an important secondary theme in the book: an interest in language and the way it can be used to obscure rather than to clarify. The officialese in which communications from the employers are couched obscures the human suffering that is involved; the 'work force' is an amount of material like ore and soil. Work is 'rationalised' to the point of calculating the time it takes for a pair of eyes to move from one object to another, but the owner of those eyes is not mentioned. Some of the workers themselves realise how they are manipulated by language and how easy it is for them to see themselves as objects if they agree to use the same language.

Å andra sidan är det ingen vinst när vi arbetare rör oss med företagets vokabulär. När vi säger *arbetskraft* om oss själva i

stället för *arbetare*. . . . När dom fått oss att säga *friställd* och
omskolning och *nedbringande av arbetskraftskostnaderna*. . . . Vil-
ken triumf för arbetsgivarna! Men om vi inte uttrycker oss så
utan försöker säga nåt av oss själva, då blir dom förnärmade.

(p. 78)

(*On the other hand, it doesn't help matters if we workers use the
vocabulary of the employers. When we say* work force *about our-
selves instead of* workers. . . . *When they get us to say* released from
employment *and* redeployment *and* improvement of cost-
effectiveness. . . . What a triumph for the employers! But if we don't
use words like that, but try instead to say something in our own way,
then they get all offended.*)

Concern for the implications of language and the tricks that can be
played with it is evident too in Sara Lidman's next book, *Vänner och
u-vänner* (1969), a collection of her articles written between 1964 and
1968. She exposes the biased assumptions behind the pro-American
newspaper reports of the Vietnam war (*USA och vårt omdöme*) and the
preference for 'neutral' phrases which disguise the fact that people are
actually being killed (*En talesman för Guam med flera*.) Ever since her
African novels Sara Lindman has tried to provoke awareness of the
realities that can be concealed under convenient labels. Thus in *Jag
och min son* the narrator is brought unwillingly face to face with the
reality he has tried to pigeon-hole, in the shape of a little child.

Så länge man inte ser dem ryms de fint i ordet *rasproblem* så fort
man ser dem har de armar och ben och ögon och allehanda
mänskliga kännetecken som gör dem svårhanterliga i ett
räknestycke.

(p. 31)

(*As long as you can't see them, you can tidy them neatly away under
the heading of* race problem; *but as soon as you see them they've got
arms and legs and eyes and all sorts of human features which makes it
difficult to think of them as mere statistics.*)

'To make it difficult to think of them as mere statistics' is the main aim
of Sara Lidman's writings.

Conclusion

This discussion has of necessity been extremely selective in terms both of the periods covered and of the authors described. To do justice to three related but distinct national literatures would be impossible even in a long book. In deciding to divide my attention between two different periods, I am aware that I have given a full picture of neither; an account of the literary debate in Sweden during the immediate post-war period and of that in Norway and Denmark during the 1960s might be thought desirable in order to give a rounded picture of the two generations of writers. But I have thought it more important to highlight those areas which provide the best examples of different kinds of political literature – periods which, as well as being of great intrinsic interest, reveal their characteristics most clearly through their contrasts. The literature of the Second World War in Norway and Denmark, with the exception of Resistance literature proper, which was copied and distributed during the occupation as a spur to action, is a literature published after the event, in which the emphasis is on reflection and on analysis of what went wrong: not that it passively accepts the present state of things, but its protest frequently looks backwards rather than forwards. And it is still fiction, for, with few exceptions, authors writing during the 1940s and early 1950s expressed themselves in the traditional literary forms. Even the Communist writers, the most ardently committed and indignant of all, clothed their most vociferous attacks in sustained fictional form.

It is otherwise with the younger Swedish (and many of the Norwegian and Danish) writers of the later period. The theme of most committed authors in the latter part of the 1960s is the present and, more urgently, the future state of society. They are not concerned, except incidentally, with apportioning blame for the past; the task is to shape the course of things to come. And not only the accepted political system but the accepted literary forms themselves come under attack as the authors try to reach beyond 'the reading public' and move from the haven of the cultural pages to more influential areas of the press. Some have abandoned fiction altogether, seeing it as an obstruction to, rather than a medium for, their meaning; others have adapted and added new elements until the novel reads more like a report, an inventory or a set of instructions. Fiction of a more traditional kind is of course still being written; but in the work of the more radical authors the priorities have been reversed. Literature no longer absorbs and purifies the base political content; insistent political conviction demands a rethinking of the basic assumptions of creative literature.

Bibliography

References are to first editions unless otherwise stated

NORWAY

General

BIRKELAND, B. og Ugelvik Larsen, S. (eds.), *Nazismen og norsk litteratur*, Bergen, 1975

BRINCHMANN, A. og Evensmo, S., *Norske forfattere i krig og fred*, Oslo, 1968

BRYNILDSEN, Å., *Fornuft og besettelse*, Oslo, 1963

BULL, F., *Tretten taler på Grini*, Oslo, 1965

DAHL, H. F. (ed.), *Fascismen i Norge 1920-40*, Kontrast No.3, 1966

LONGUM, L., *Frontlinjer*, Oslo, 1966

LONGUM, L., *Et speil for oss selv*, Oslo, 1968

NORENG, H. (ed.), *Den moderne roman og romanforskning i Norden*, Bergen, 1971

NOTAKER, H. (ed.), *Reis ingen monumenter*, (*Lyrikk fra okkupasjonstiden*), Oslo, 1969

STAI, A., *Norsk kultur- og moraldebatt i 1930-årene*, Oslo, 1954

SØRGAARD, N-A., *Fire forfattere og norsk fascisme*, Oslo, 1973

Individual authors

GRIEG, N., *Vår ære og vår makt*, Gyldendals skoleutgave, Oslo, 1963

GRIEG, N., *Nederlaget*, Gyldendals skoleutgave, 2nd edition, Oslo, 1962

GRIEG, N., *Ung må verden ennu være*, 7th edition, Oslo, 1962

GRIEG, N., *Samlede dikt*, Oslo, 1966

EGELAND, K., *Nordahl Grieg*, Oslo, 1953

HASLUND, F. J., *Nordahl Grieg*, Oslo, 1962

VESAAS, T., *Ultimatum*, Oslo, 1934

VESAAS, T., *Kimen*, Den norske bokklubben, Oslo, 1967

VESAAS, T., *Huset i mørkret*, Gyldendals lanterne-bøker, Oslo, 1970

BEYER, E., *et al*, *Tarjei Vesaas 1897-1967*, Oslo, 1967

BROSTRØM, T., 'Tarjei Vesaas' symbolverden belyst ud fra hans prosaverker 1940-50'. *Edda*, vol 55, 1955

CHAPMAN, K., *Hovedlinjer i Tarjei Vesaas' diktning*, Oslo, 1969 (also published in English in Twayne's World Authors Series, New York, 1970)

HOEL, S., *Sesam, Sesam*, Samlede romaner og fortellinger, Oslo, 1950

HOEL, S., *Tanker i mørketid*, Oslo, 1945

HOEL, S., *Møte ved milepelen*, 5th edition, Oslo, 1964

HOEL, S., *Stevnemøte med glemte år*, Oslo, 1954

EGELAND, K., *Skyld og skjebne*. Oslo, 1960

HANNEVIK, A., 'Kjærligheten og trollringen — noen grunnmotiver i Sigurd Hoels diktning'. *Ord och Bild*, vol 70, 1961

HAALAND, A., *Hamsun og Hoel*, Bergen, 1957

INADOMI, M., *Den plettfrie*. En analyse av Sigurd Hoels *Møte ved milepelen*, Halden, 1968

TVINNEREIM, A., *Risens hjerte – en studie i Sigurd Hoels forfatterskap*, Oslo, 1975

DENMARK

General

ALKIL, N. (ed.), *Besættelsestidens fakta I-II*, Copenhagen, 1945

BUSCHARDT, L., Fabritius, A., og Tønnesen, H., *Besættelsestidens illegale blade og bøger*, Copenhagen, 1954

Der brænder en Ild, Anthology, Folk og Frihed, 1944

HERTEL, H. (ed.), *Tilbageblik paa 30'erne I-II*, Copenhagen, 1967

HÆSTRUP, J. (ed.), *Besættelsens hvem-hvad-hvor*, Copenhagen, 1966

KRISTENSEN, S. M., 'Kunst og politik før og efter krigen', in *Litteratur-sociologiske essays*, Copenhagen, 1968

MADSEN, C., *Den gode Læge*, 4th edition, Copenhagen, 1968

MADSEN, C., *Vi skrev Loven*, Copenhagen, 1968

WAMBERG, N. B. (ed.), *Samtaler med danske Digtere*, Copenhagen, 1968

WIVEL, O., *Poesi og protest*, Copenhagen, 1971

Individual authors
MUNK, K., *Mindeudgave*, Copenhagen, 1949, vol II, *Dagen er inde og andre Artikler*, vol III, *Digte*, vol V, *Egelykke og andre Skuespil*

HENRIQUES, Alf, *Kaj Munk*, Copenhagen, 1945

KIRK, H., *Daglejerne*, 8th edition, Copenhagen, 1965

KIRK, H., *De ny Tider*, 3rd edition, Copenhagen, 1971

KIRK, H., *Slaven*, 2nd edition, Copenhagen, 1966

KIRK, H., *Vredens Søn*, 2nd edition, Copenhagen, 1969

KIRK, H., *Djævelens Penge*, Vintens forlag, Copenhagen, 1967

KIRK, H., *Klitgaard og Sønner*, Vintens forlag, Copenhagen, 1969

KIRK, H., *Fange Nr.6 – Breve fra Horserød*, Odense, 1967

ANDERSEN, J. K. og Emerek, L., *Hans Kirks forfatterskab*, Copenhagen, 1972

SCHERFIG, H., *Den forsvundne Fuldmægtig*, 9th edition, Copenhagen, 1969

SCHERFIG, H., *Det forsømte Forår*, 10th edition, Copenhagen, 1965

SCHERFIG, H., *Idealister*, 5th edition, Copenhagen, 1966

SCHERFIG, H., *Frydenholm*, 3rd edition, Copenhagen, 1966

ANDERSEN, J. K. og Emerek, L., *Hans Scherfigs forfatterskab*, Copenhagen, 1973

BREDSDORFF, E., 'Hans Scherfigs Frydenholm', in *Den moderne roman og romanforskning i Norden*, Bergen, 1971

CLANTE, C., *Normale mennesker, Hans Scherfig og hans romaner*, Copenhagen, 1975

JOOST, V., *Scherfig*, Aalborg, 1974

BRANNER, H. C., *Fem Radiospil*, Copenhagen, 1965

BRANNER, H. C., *Legetøj*, 7th edition, Copenhagen, 1969

BRANNER, H. C., *Om lidt er vi borte*, 5th edition, Copenhagen, 1944

BRANNER, H. C., *Angst*, Copenhagen, 1947

BRANNER, H. C., *Bjergene*, Copenhagen, 1953

BRANNER, H. C., *Ingen kender Natten*, 5th edition, Copenhagen, 1965

BRANNER, H. C., *Røde Heste i Sneen*, anthology, Copenhagen, 1962

BORGEN, J., 'H. C. Branner', *Vinduet*, 1962

FREDERIKSEN, E., *H. C. Branner*, Copenhagen, 1966

VOSMAR, J., *H. C. Branner*, Copenhagen, 1959

MARKEY, T. L., *H. C. Branner*, New York, 1973

HANSEN, M. A., *Jonatans Rejse*, 4th edition, Copenhagen, 1961

HANSEN, M. A., *Lykkelige Kristoffer*, 8th edition, Copenhagen, 1967

HANSEN, M. A., *Tornebusken*, 4th edition, Copenhagen, 1955

HANSEN, M. A., *Agerhønen*, 8th edition, Copenhagen, 1966

BJØRNVIG, T., *Kains Alter*, Copenhagen, 1965

BJØRNVIG, T., *Forsvar for Kains Alter*, Copenhagen, 1965

INGWERSEN, F. and N., *Martin A. Hansen*, Boston, 1976

WIVEL, O., *Martin A. Hansen*, vol I, Copenhagen, 1967, vol II, Copenhagen, 1969

SWEDEN

General

Bonniers Litterära Magasin 1970, No I, *Backspeglar på sextiotalet*

BRANTING, J., Håkanson, B., och Sundberg, K. (eds.), *29 röster-67*, Stockholm, 1967

BROSTRØM, T., *Moderne svensk litteratur*, Copenhagen, 1973
BÄCKSTRÖM, L., *Litteraturpolitik*, Uddevalla, 1970
ENQUIST, P. O. (ed.), *Sextiotalskritik*, Stockholm, 1966
ENQUIST, P. O., 'Eight Parentheses on Swedish Moods', in 'Scandinavian Writing Today', *Times Literary Supplement*, 10/9/71
FRANZÉN, L-O., *Omskrivningar*, Uddevalla, 1968
FREDRIKSSON, G., *Det politiska språket*, Lund, 1972
GYLLENSTEN, L., *Nihilistiskt credo*, Stockholm, 1964
HALLBERG, P., 'Dokument – engagemang – fiktion', in *Nordisk tidsskrift*, 1970
HÅKANSON, B., *Författarmakt, Inlägg och essäer om litterature i politik och politik i litteraturen*, Stockholm, 1970
HÅKANSON, B., och Nylén, L. (eds.), *Nya linjer. Lyrik från 60-talet* (v. introduction), Stockholm, 1966
LAGERLÖF, K. E., *Samtal med 60-talister*, Stockholm, 1965
LINDQVIST, S., *Självklara saker*, Stockholm, 1970
NILSSON, S., och Yrlid, R., *Svensk litteratur i kritik och debatt 1957-70*, Stockholm, 1972
PRINTZ-PÅHLSON, G., *Förtroendekrisen*, Artiklar och debattinlägg 1958-1970, Stockholm, 1971
PRINTZ-PÅHLSON, G., *Slutna världar öppen rymd*, Essäer och kritiker 1956-1971, Stockholm, 1971
SWAHN, S., 'Attitudes to Literature in Sweden in the Sixties', *Scandinavica*, supplement to vol 12, no. I, May 1973
Tryckpunkter, 23 svenska författare i egen sak, Stockholm, 1967

Individual authors
ENQUIST, P. O. *Magnetisörens femte vinter*, Stockholm, 1964
ENQUIST, P. O., *Hess*, 2nd edition, Stockholm, 1968
ENQUIST, P. O., *Legionärerna*, Stockholm, 1970
ENQUIST, P. O., *Sekonden*, Stockholm, 1971
'Enkät: Löper den politiskt orienterade författaren en särskild risk att hamna i abstraktioner?', *BLM* no. 2, 1968
LINNÉR, S., 'Per Olov Enquists Legionärerna', in *Den moderne roman og romanforskning i Norden*, Bergen, 1971

SONNEVI, G., *Det gäller oss* (includes *Outfört, Abstrakta dikter, ingrepp-modeller, och nu!*), Stockholm, 1969
SONNEVI, G., *Det måste gå*, Stockholm, 1970
SONNEVI, G., *Det oavslutade språket*, Stockholm, 1972

MYRDAL, J., *Två folkhemsromaner (Jubelvår, Badrumskranen)*, Stockholm, 1968
MYRDAL, J., *Rapport från kinesisk by*, Stockholm, 1963

MYRDAL, J., *Samtida*, Stockholm, 1967

MYRDAL, J., *Moraliteter*, Stockholm, 1967

MYRDAL, J., *Skriftställning*, Stockholm, 1968

THYGESEN, M., *Jan Myrdal og Sara Lidman, Rapportgenren i svensk 60-tals litteratur*, Århus, 1971

LIDMAN, S., *Jag och min son*, Delfinserien, Bonniers, Stockholm, 1971

LIDMAN, S., *Med fem diamanter*, Stockholm, 1964

LIDMAN, S., *Samtal i Hanoi*, Delfinserien, 2nd edition, Stockholm, 1971

LIDMAN, S., *Gruva*, Aldusserien, Bonniers, 3rd edition, Stockholm, 1970

LIDMAN, S., *Vänner och u-vänner*, Stockholm, 1969

LINDQVIST, S., 'En löjlig människas dröm', in *Självklara saker*, Stockholm, 1970

THORELL, G., 'Samtal med Sara', *Ord och Bild* no. I, 1970

THYGESEN, M., *Jan Myrdal og Sara Lidman, Rapportgenren i svensk 60-tals litteratur*, Århus, 1971